MOVING THE MOUNTAIN

MOVING THE
MOUNTAIN

Ronald Mann

Aldersgate Productions

First published 1995
by Aldersgate Productions Ltd
12 Palace Street
London SW1E 5JF

© Ronald Mann

ISBN 0 9525077 01

British Library Cataloguing-in-publication Data:
A catalogue record of this book is available
from the British Library.

Designed and typeset by Blair Cummock
Cover design by Dell Williams

Printed by Biddles Ltd, Guildford, England

Contents

Illustrations

COLOUR PLATES

Acknowledgements

I AM extremely grateful to John Goulding who took my first rough draft and helped me to turn it into a book, and to Elizabeth Locke who did some superb editing of the final script.

In order to canvass reaction to my book I showed the manuscript to many friends, some of whom had known me for many years and others just a short time. So many thanks to Louis Fleming, Rob and Jacqui Frost, John and Sheila Gibbs, Nigel and Gillie Goodwin, Stanley Kiaer, Will Kneale, Paul and Nancy Lang, Hugh Nowell, Ann Warren, Hugh and Dell Williams. Even if their suggestions were sometimes contradictory, they were a great help and encouragement.

I am grateful to Dell Williams for the cover design, for help with picture research and with publicity; to Blair Cummock for the design and production; to Paul Remouf for the colour transparencies, and to Janet Smith for the proof reading.

Carolyn Spalding over a period of 18 months patiently typed my many, many drafts and had the great skill of being able to read my writing. She was very encouraging in those decisive early stages, for all of which I am grateful.

My special thanks to Dr Donald Coggan for writing the foreword.

Foreword

IF YOU WANT a good read, you will find it here. The story of the writer as a prisoner of war, escaping over the Italian mountains, is in itself an exciting saga. But *Moving the Mountain* is much more that this. It is a story of spiritual birth and growth; of obedience to God's guidance as he makes his will known to a listening disciple; of friendships with people in all walks of life and in all parts of the world.

Ronald Mann's life has been – and is – one of intense activity, but he is no workaholic. His life has been enriched by his partnership of 40 years with his wife Mary and with his son John, and by his passion for painting. He is a great lover of nature and especially of the mountains – he can hardly keep away from the Lake District. His painting provides relaxation but he also views it as a way of expressing the wonder he feels.

He is driven by a passion – to share with others the riches which he has found in the Christian way of life. He longs that the Christian voice should be heard in all the media. Too many, he feels, are slow 'to provide first-class professional theatre which conveys Christian truth in such a way that it can entertain, enlighten, educate, and open the door to faith'. He wants to help our generation to find its soul. With that end in view, he envisages a steady production of plays which portray the deepest truths about a human being's journey through life. The media must be penetrated, in all its forms, by those insights without which human beings cannot live *whole* lives, cannot achieve their destiny. Why not the establishment of a Christian Arts Centre in London – 'a centre where new writers can be found, new productions encouraged', outreach to the media at home and abroad made possible? Mountains are there not *only* to be painted. Sometimes they are there to be moved. Sometimes to be tunnelled through.

Got any rivers you think are uncrossable?
Got any mountains you can't tunnel through?
We specialise in the wholly impossible.
Doing the things that no man can do.
Ronald is one of those specialists.

Donald Coggan

ix

Introduction

I HAVE written this book for the thousand or more people who have bought my paintings and for those who have seen the plays I've promoted or produced – who must now number more than two million – and also for a great many of my other friends, as well as for the general public.

I wanted them to know more of my journey. It is the journey of someone from a small town on the north Lancashire coast who left school before his 17th birthday, and who has been led into the most extraordinary adventures, and into areas of life he would never have dreamt of.

The book is dedicated to all those who've been my companions in these adventures, and also to Heaton Cooper who taught me how to paint, and to my wife Mary who inspired me to live life to the full.

PART I
THE WAR YEARS

Chapter 1 ADVENTURE

'GOD BLESS YOU,' said the Franciscan as he turned to leave us at the start of the mountain track. He had led us from the prison hospital in Piacenza in northern Italy, through the Appennine village of Bettola and over a small bridge. 'Well, here you are,' he said. 'I think you'll find the mountain people friendly. Now it's up to you.'

That was a moment I'll never forget. The sound of running water, the scent of the trees and mountain air, and above all the fact that after 18 months in prison camps I was free. It was breathtaking. I felt the same kind of excitement that I had had as a child arriving for summer holidays at a new seaside town, eager to rush to the nearest beach. I was indeed 'surprised by joy'. In fact every time I tell of my escape, and that has been scores of times, I find that a lump comes in my throat remembering the sheer wonder of that moment.

It didn't matter that I was still in occupied territory and might be hunted down, recaptured, even shot. What mattered was that I was free and able to make my own decisions.

This arrival in the mountains was even more startling because, for almost a year before being taken prisoner, I'd been in the Western Desert. Although I loved the cleanness of the air and light there, and the sense of space, and the occasional delight of seeing a carpet of small flowers after a heavy dew, I did long for trees, mountains and running water.

THE WESTERN DESERT

I had joined the army in March 1940 as an ordinary private and been commissioned in the Royal Artillery in December of that year. By August of 1941 I was commanding a troop of anti-tank guns in the Libyan desert, but I was very inexperienced and knew it. The other commander was George Dunkerley who became a lifelong friend.

If you have to fight a war, a desert is not a bad place to do it; there are no civilians and there is a certain spirit in

In the army

the battle which makes it almost a game – although a dangerous one.

It was a time when we were very short of material, and the nearest British tanks were two or three hundred miles behind us. We were part of a formation of fast moving columns whose task was to move rapidly against the enemy, often behind his position, mount a quick attack and then move away again.

One tactic we used against the German tanks was to lie behind the sandhills with our anti-tank guns, wait until they were near enough for us to do some damage, and

After training, he was drafted to a mountain regiment preparing in Palestine with horses and mules for Greece. As Greece was overrun before the regiment was ready, he was transferred to the Northumberland Hussars – anti-tank gunners.

4

then retreat with our guns, which were mounted on powerful trucks, and rely on the cloud of dust we created to protect us from the fire of their tanks.

It was on one of these manoeuvres that the truck I was on suddenly broke down, when the German tanks were just a hundred yards away on the other side of a sandhill. Not being in a position to take on a troop of tanks with one two-pounder gun, we removed the gun mechanism and ran to try and hide in some of the desert shrubs. These however proved inadequate cover and very soon we were being rounded up and taken prisoner. This was March 1943.

PRISONER OF WAR

A few months later I wrote in my diary, 'There is no describing the sickening and deadening sensation of being taken prisoner. One minute you are living in an active familiar world, granted a somewhat perilous one, and suddenly within the space of a few minutes (in my case seconds) everything is changed. You then see everything from the other side, and instead of watching the German tanks advancing, you are following on behind them. You are now with the Germans against whom you have been fighting and can talk with them. One of them said, "Bad luck being caught; I got caught last week but got away, but don't you try that," while others crowed, "Caught you on the run this time."

'But it is not the fact of being on the other side of the battle, or of meeting your enemies that strikes you most. It is the change from action to in-action, the change from giving orders to being carried about, not even ordered, but just moved like a load of ammunition or a bundle of empty petrol tins. Then there is the sickening game of "if", day in and day out, and especially night in and night out. You live the last scene over and over again. I pictured how it might have been if only I had given a different order, if I had only placed No 3 gun in a different position, if only that wretched half shaft on the truck had not broken, or had broken half a minute earlier or later, if only this or that.'

In the following months dreams of 'if only' went on and on, alternating with the thought of escape – both the escapes I might have made had I seized the available chances, generally rather wild ones, and the escape I was going to make. It was many years later that I realised the

5

truth that although God doesn't ordain everything that happens to us, He seems to allow it. This removes the 'if only' from one's life forever and you can accept whatever God gives for the present and for the future.

The next three months were fairly rough – sometimes riding in the back of a German three-ton lorry over the rough desert tracks in a blazing sun – sometimes trying to sleep in a derelict fort on its bug-infested floor – always looking for the chance to escape, but never finding a good enough opportunity.

Eventually we arrived at Tripoli, Libya, where for three months we lived in a provisional transit camp on the edge of the desert waiting to be shipped to Italy.

I asked the British medical officer who was a fellow prisoner with us, 'What causes malnutrition?' He replied, 'Just carry on with the present diet for a few more weeks, and you'll have first hand experience of it.' We were given a piece of coarse bread and ersatz coffee for breakfast, a very thin soup for lunch, and in the evening a piece of very gristly meat. Every day we saw a herd of donkeys driven past the camp, and the story was that each day there was one less, the herd being the source of our supper. It might have been true, as I've never seen meat like it.

The only addition to this was that we could get dates from the local Arabs, and these we used to boil up with the bread ration, producing a wonderfully soggy pudding which made us feel better for a short time.

There was one book in the camp, and so in an afternoon one could sit along a wall and pass the loose pages of the book along the line of prisoners who had decided to spend the afternoon in this way. It wasn't a very interesting book. We also improvised a chess board and bits of tile marked with the names of the pieces and spent hours playing chess. Another occupation was watching the bull ants fight with a dung beetle. Eventually the ants, although much smaller, won by sheer weight of numbers.

In the room I shared with eight other officers, another pastime was drawing on the walls a map of the West End of London, with which some of them were very familiar, possibly too familiar. As I had only been to London twice in my life, I could only watch with interest and study that part of London where I was to live some years later.

During this time I got dysentery. This was agonising as I had to stand on a chair by the window to attract the attention of the sentry, who went past every few minutes, to let me out and escort me to the latrine – also a somewhat

6

primitive affair. However, after becoming somewhat delirious I was moved to a hospital wing and taken better care of.

After the three months we were put into the hold of a German cargo ship, with a hard biscuit (which we discovered was full of weevils) as rations, and set sail for Italy. During the night there seemed to be some commotion on the decks, and we sensed that the ship was changing direction. Eventually the engines stopped, and we guessed that we were in a harbour – probably Tunis. We searched for ways to open the big doors of the hold with wild ideas of getting out and swimming for the shore. It's probably a good thing that we didn't succeed, as in our weakened state it's doubtful whether we would have been able to swim very far.

NAPLES

So it was after three days, instead of the 24 hour trip we'd expected, that we arrived in Naples harbour somewhat hungry and certainly very dirty.

We were shepherded across the quay under the curious gaze of passers-by and on to a train, and then transported a few kilometres to another transit camp at Capua. There we joined other prisoners. In our compound we were about 200 officers crowded into four wooden huts in a space about 60 yards by 20 yards. We stayed here for another three months.

The main feature of this camp was that it was inhabited by the largest imaginable population of bed bugs. They would leave a line of bite marks on your legs if you were sitting on a chair, and at night creep out of the bed boards and attack you where they could, even dropping from the ceiling to join in the fun. We used to take the bed boards out during the day time and burn out of them with a match both the bugs and the eggs they had laid, but this gave a respite for a few days only.

We longed to get to a more permanent camp and also constantly thought of ways to escape. One plan I had was a very wild one. I would simply walk out through the main entrance during the night, when the sentry sat down and often dozed. I would make for the outer fence, which never seemed to be guarded nor looked particularly difficult to get through, and then once outside find a way back to Naples and board a neutral ship.

Fortunately for me three others planned and executed a

similar plan before I did, with disastrous results. They fused some of the lights and got through the gates past the dozing sentry, but the two who reached the perimeter fence were caught and shot by a patrol. We had reason to believe that word had got out of their attempt and that a patrol had been specially placed on the outside. The third man who planned to go, Gordon Clover, got to the gate as the sentry woke up, and so turned back in time and was safely in bed when the guards and officers came charging round. One of the two men who got out died immediately and the other a few hours later.

The prisoner of war experience was a mixture of being cramped, restricted and hungry. It also meant an expanding of horizons, as I met and lived close to people whom I wouldn't normally have got to know. For the Red Cross parcels distribution, which were a lifeline for us, we organised ourselves into 'syndicates' of five to share each parcel. We became very expert in dividing a piece of cheese, for instance, into five equal segments. We used to have the rule that the person who did the dividing had the last choice of pieces. It was amazing how accurate we became.

The syndicates themselves were great discussion centres, as we spent much time together. At one point in our syndicate there was a national trade union official, a stockbroker who later became a member of parliament, a very sophisticated and charming man from a theatrical family, and a barrister who later became a judge. The barrister would always take the weakest side in the argument whatever his own view was, in order to make it interesting and lively. I gained an insight into both other people's lives and their ways of thinking that I would never have got in ordinary everyday life.

I learned here also how concentrated the mind could become on food. There was always great excitement when the canteen was opened. Under Red Cross regulations we were paid a certain number of lire, and we could buy at the canteen a rationed number of figgy bars, a confectionery of flour and figs. They became available only occasionally, and one of our number used to hoard them and then sell them at a profit later.

This so aroused the indignation of the rest of the camp that this man, who was the senior officer in the camp responsible for negotiating with the Italian commandant, was voted out of the position, and we elected someone else in his place.

The other commodity one could buy at certain times

were the most delicious peaches. So a diet of a small piece of bread and fairly meagre other rations could be supplemented by a kilo, or sometimes more, of ripe peaches. You can imagine the effect on our insides.

REZZONELLO

After three months confined in this compound, we were at last taken to the north of Italy, to a place called Rezzonello in the hills near Piacenza where there were 150 officers and 150 other ranks. It was a castle, 200 years old, built in the form of a square with a quadrangle in the centre, and at each corner of the square a small tower. Previously it had been a nunnery, and our life within it could be compared to the monastic life. All connection with the outside was severed. Our only links were letters, the Italian officers and interpreters, an occasional wireless programme, and guarded walks through the country lanes. Our food was sparse enough for any ascetic, and our occupation for the most part study, lectures, reading and an occasional concert.

A prison camp is a separate community, and like all communities we had our head man, our committees for this and for that, our representatives, and our own laws and regulations. You might think that in such a restricted life rules would be unnecessary, but on the contrary, the more restricted and difficult the conditions, the more people are tempted to be anti-social and to grasp that little bit extra for themselves.

Another aspect that stands out in my memory is the mass feeling. I remember a batch of 20 officers coming in from another camp, all fairly recently captured, and all feeling very optimistic. It was only a matter of hours before the whole camp was expecting to be free within a very short time (with the exception of certain die-hards). A little bit of news, a good rumour, and the whole camp would begin to buzz. At one time five naval officers were sent away to be repatriated, and you could hear the hum of conversation, little groups of people talking, and the first words of the conversation were – 'What do you think of it?' or 'Have you heard what the Italian sanitary orderly said?' In the space of two or three days the excitement rose to a terrific pitch, then as suddenly as it had started, finished, and reaction set in. Rumours came in frequently of political activity in Italy that led us to believe that the Fascists were losing control, but so many rumours were

9

proved unfounded that one scarcely knew what to believe.

At times I settled down to prison life, filling the day with study, and lived contentedly, but the possibility and hope of escape were always there. The greatest heartache was to look out at the wonderful Italian mountains and countryside and not to be able to explore them, and of course the longing rose to walk again in my beloved Lakeland hills. Several times the Lombardy plain below us was covered in the mist and in the far distance above the mist we could see the Alps shining in sunlight.

A secret I had learnt before the war from one of our Methodist ministers who had met the Oxford Group was that in any circumstances one could seek and find the Holy Spirit. This was a wonderful secret to have learnt which has been very important for me throughout my life. So every day I would take a few minutes on my own, in a quiet corner if I could find one, and note down on a scrap of paper any thoughts that came. They weren't particularly illuminating, but they did give a certain direction and purpose to life, and one idea – that I should learn Italian – proved to be very important later on.

The Italian authorities allowed a rotund and delightful, although somewhat scruffy, Italian priest to come into the camp to teach us his language. He was a very good teacher and would pointedly mock and imitate our horrible pronunciation. 'You massacre my beautiful language!' he would sorrowfully cry. Eventually, because he was always maligning the Fascists, the authorities banned him from coming any more, but at least he'd given us the foundation.

Suddenly one day we heard that we were moving, and within a week we were in another camp for 600 officers. The camp had been an orphanage in peace time and was in the middle of the village of Fontanellato, near Parma; we could watch ordinary life going on outside the wire.

FONTANELLATO

This was a well organised camp; the food from the Red Cross was pooled, and made a part of our regular meals, apart from the chocolate and soap which we divided amongst us. Our life could most easily be compared to a cross between a university and a monastery.

I'd been brought up in the atmosphere of a good home, very much based on what is often called the 'Protestant ethic'. To work hard, to study to achieve, to advance

10

oneself in the world was a moral duty. So my life before the war was made up of working hard every day, including Saturday mornings, in the County Offices at Preston. Studying every evening as soon as I got home with a correspondence course, playing rugby every Saturday afternoon or tennis in the summer, and spending Sunday at church and with my friends.

There was no time at all for reading or much entertainment apart from church functions and occasional amateur dramatics. It was a hard working life without much space for the wider interests of literature, art, and music. In fact people who did become keen on these things were regarded as just a little bit odd.

In prison camp leisure was all we had, and so I began to taste the other riches of life beyond my career, attending lectures on a wide variety of subjects. In a camp of 600 officers, there were people with a wide range of knowledge and experience. I remember being fascinated by lectures that a regular army officer, an Oxford Greats scholar, gave over several weeks on Plato's *Republic*.

We also had our own art study group. There were two good professional artists who led our group, and we had amongst other things life classes and lessons in different painting techniques. From my school days I had always been very keen on painting, and so even in the first camp I would do pencil sketches of my fellow prisoners.

At this camp we were able to obtain water-colours and oils, and as well as the classes I began to concentrate on portraits. Everyone was delighted to sit for as long as I wished, so there were plenty of subjects. I used to choose whom I would like to paint and then watch him on the roll calls (which generally lasted three quarters of an hour) before finally deciding from which particular angle I would paint him and what I would try to portray of his character.

I lost sight of all these paintings when I escaped, but an oil painting of the scene out of the windows of the building at Fontanellato came back to me in a remarkable way. In 1944 I was staying for the weekend in the home of the fellow officer, Jasper Kerr, who had been in the prison hospital with me. (I had been moved there because I had badly damaged my right eye during a football game.)

Jasper had been repatriated because he had tuberculosis very badly, and was at that time in a sanatorium. As the conversation turned to painting one of his parents said, 'I wonder if you know anything about a painting we found in the bottom of Jasper's suitcase?' and then produced it. It was my landscape in oils. Jasper had carried it with him to Germany and then back to England. He must have found it amongst the things I'd left behind when I escaped. I still have that painting.

At Fontanellato we were allowed access to a playing field near to the camp. It was surrounded by barbed wire and guards, but every evening it was closed, and we were ushered back into the main building. We got permission to level the ground for a basketball field and were given spades to do this with.

Another aspect of the good organisation at Fontanellato was that there was just one officer responsible for co-ordinating any escape attempts, in the same way that one saw in the film *The Great Escape*.

Five men had approached him with a scheme involving this playing field. While levelling the pitch they dug a large hole, put in it two or three planks they'd obtained in order to help level the pitch, and then covered them with soil and put great lumps of the clay soil at the end. As roll call was signalled, some of us were enlisted to play with a ball in front of the various sentries whilst two men, shielded by our antics in front of the sentries, crawled into the hole and stayed there until the field was shut off. The sentries inspected the field, walking near the hole, but saw nothing unusual as it had been well covered.

When it was dark several hours later, they got out under the barbed wire, there being no sentries then on the outside of the field. These two travelled by night and got as far as Lake Como, within sight of the frontier with Switzerland, before they were caught.

The roll call was fudged by having two of the officers pretending to lie sick in bed in one wing. When the Italian officer had counted them, he would check the other floors in that wing and then take the passage at the top of the building to the other wing. Meanwhile, these two would quickly go down to the basement and cross to the other wing, get into bed with some other complaint and so be counted twice.

The following day three hid in the hole. Two got through the wire, and when the third didn't arrive at the agreed point they went on and, having forged papers as Spanish workmen, succeeded in getting on the train for the north. The third man had ripped his clothes on the barbed wire, and when he got to the station later he aroused suspicion. The railway police got in touch with our camp, a roll call was quickly taken, and it was discovered then that

12

Reproduction of the author's oil painting from inside the prison camp at Fontanellato

there were five men missing. Word was sent up the line, and the two who had gone ahead were questioned again. They almost convinced the police at the station that they were Spanish workers, but as they were walking out of the office they were called back while the police checked with our camp, and so were recaptured.

Towards the summer of 1943 expectancy in the camp began to rise. First there was the Allied landing in Sicily, and after its completion the hope of a landing in Italy was always before us. Then there was the constant buzz of political activity and unrest in the country which eventually led to the overthrow of Mussolini. I remember the morning very well when someone came into the room very early and said Mussolini had gone. Only two or three were up at the time, but it was not long before everyone was sitting up in bed and discussing what they thought was a new rumour.

I went to the side of the building facing the Italian parade ground, and it was immediately obvious that something had happened. The Italians were standing about in small groups, and every time an officer appeared there was a stir of excitement and expectancy. It was not long before the radio loudspeaker in the square was turned on, and everyone waited excitedly for the news.

There were two messages, one from Badoglio and the other from the King, Victor Emmanuel III. The new regime was announced with Badoglio at the head of the government. The Italians were more excited than we were, singing and shouting, and all the Fascist slogans

13

with which Mussolini had covered the walls of the villages were quickly erased, whilst any pictures or statues of Mussolini were dealt with by fire or black paint.

But there was no mention of an armistice or of us being released. The fact was that on the whole the Italian people were disillusioned and tired of the war and their alliance with Germany.

On 2nd September 1943, whilst playing football, I damaged my right eye and was sent to the prison hospital in Piacenza. The first week I spent there was rather like watching an exciting film when you have a violent toothache. The outside events were fascinating, but it was hard to force my attention on them as my eye and cheek were swollen and painful. I had lost the sight of my right eye and using one eye by itself was a tiring and irritating business. All the same I have a very clear recollection of the evening of the 8th.

Jasper Kerr and I shared one room. Another officer, called George, and the padre were in the next room. George, a very excitable chap, came dashing into our room with the words, 'They've signed an armistice' and was simply frothing at the mouth. He was followed very quickly by a Yugoslav major who was even more excited and much more unreliable. As our only means of conversation with the Yugoslav was in French and Italian, both of which he spoke very inadequately, he had to content himself with embracing Jasper and gurgling away in a mixture of French, Italian and Serbo-Croat.

Jasper and I were slow to believe, but when we heard the sound of singing and cheering in the streets we were convinced. We hardly knew what to do, as it seemed that at last we were free. I remember Jasper saying, 'But it can't happen like this' – the moment we had been waiting for this last year and a half.

We were too excited to sleep much that night; we listened to the singing and shouting in the streets, and we wondered how long it would take our troops to reach us, perhaps ten days or a fortnight. Stories came through of landings by the Allies and practically every port was mentioned – Naples, Genoa, Spezia, Livorno and so on. Would the Germans fight a strong rearguard or get out quickly? We did not think that they would have time to think about a little out of the way hospital like this. The camps they might take over but we felt pretty safe in this spot.

The Germans did in fact react quickly. In some POW camps where the commandant was friendly, prisoners were let out before the Germans took over. My old camp of Fontanellato was one of these. Others were less fortunate although some prisoners did escape from the trains when they were being taken to Germany. Some jumped from moving trains. Others pulled up boards and got down between the railway lines and waited there until the train moved on. The German High Command poured fresh troops into Italy. A parachute unit rescued Mussolini from the hotel high up on the Gran Sasso where he was being hidden. They quickly took control of the country, which was divided. Most people were for breaking with Germany, but a fanatical minority still clung to Mussolini and his Fascist ideas.

Very shortly they poured into Piacenza and also took over our hospital building.

One morning as I was spending a few moments quietly on my own, the thought came, 'Ask the Germans if you can go and see Robinson.' Robinson was a British soldier who had been working in our camp, and for whom the strain of prison camp had been too much. He had tried to commit suicide, and he was now being treated in a mental hospital, also in Piacenza.

Permission was given, and the next day I was driven, in the back of a well-covered truck, from our prison hospital to this mental hospital. The flap of the truck blew open and without anything particular in mind and largely out of habit, I made a mental note of the way the truck went, second right, first left, and so on.

At the mental hospital the Italian and French nuns who ran it were much more friendly towards me than towards the German guard. After a chat with the British soldier, who was somewhat better, I was driven back convinced that if I could only find a way out of the prison hospital, I could look for assistance to these nuns.

Chapter 2 ESCAPE

THREE DAYS later we found a loose bar in one of the second floor windows. Some of my friends urged caution and delay, arguing that I would be fitter later on. But we had heard rumours that we would be soon moved to Germany, and the insistent thought came into my mind, 'Go now. Go now.' In fact the camp was moved a few days later.

Jasper was eager to come, but I was very worried as he had a temperature and was far from well. I did not know at the time that he had tuberculosis. Fortunately I saw the Slav doctor about it, and he said it would be fatal for him to go and that within a few days he was quite likely to become dangerously infectious. The doctor was not keen to tell Jasper this, feeling it would not be good for him to know, but eventually because he was so determined to go with me we had to tell him. Fred Stokes, a tough Geordie guardsman, agreed to come with me.

It may seem surprising but the decision to break out of prison was a hard one. On the one hand there was the safe sad world of inside, where there was at least a bed, some food and some warmth, and a certain safety. On the other there was the danger of escape, of being killed, and the unknown hazards of cold and hunger, nowhere to sleep and no certainty or security. The hold of the known and the safe is always strong and not least in prison camp. For me, however, I was sure that this was right, and that it was God who had put the thought to go in my mind.

That evening I slipped away to the room on the second floor of the prison building where some of my friends were already making preparations. The room was in darkness, and one of my fellow prisoners was on top of two stacked tables, trying the bars at the top of the high windows. Meanwhile others quietly slipped into the dark room with sheets and began to tie them into a sheet rope. Along the corridor outside and down the stairs we had men watching to give us warning in case any of the guards inside the building should start to come in our direction.

The man balanced on top of the tables grunted and shoved – finally he whispered, 'It won't move.' He tried again and someone whispered, 'Are you sure it's the right window?' So hastily he climbed down, and we piled the tables on top of each other again, to reach the top of another of the tall windows. The same man climbed up and reached for the top horizontal bar. There was complete silence, except for his heavy breathing, and then a whispered, 'It's OK, sir – this is the one.' Quickly the sheets were knotted to the bottom bars, and then again there was a delay as we realised that they weren't long enough to reach far enough down into the courtyard below. So hurriedly, and yet unobtrusively, one man was sent to get more sheets.

It seemed an eternity as we waited without a sound in the darkness – the sergeant major who had helped me organize everything, three others including Jasper who were helping with the sheets and tables, and Fred. Quietly the door opened, and in came the man with the extra sheets. Quickly they were knotted onto the others, and one end fixed to the bar. I climbed up on to the tables, pushed my shoulder under the bar so that it moved in the plaster and I was able to squeeze my body through. For a second I hung somewhat perilously to the outside of the bars, until I was able to ease my way down and clasp hold of the sheet tied to the bar at the bottom of the window. Safely on the rope, I let myself down into the dark, silent, and unguarded courtyard.

As I got further down I swung a little on the sheet rope and with a crash that sounded to me as loud as cannon fire, my foot went into a pane of glass. A second later I touched the ground and listened intently, expecting to hear the sound of running feet and the voices of the guards. But all was quiet. A minute later Fred was on the sheet rope and slid silently down beside me. Then our packs were lowered. There was a whispered, 'Good luck,' from the window above, and we made for the entrance to the flats that used the same courtyard. As we went in, we saw the back of someone going upstairs, but he didn't turn round. We went through the entrance lobby and then opened the door onto the main street.

Knowing that the main entrance of the prison hospital was a few yards up the street, we had decided just to walk out as if we lived there, and as it was the dusk of early evening, we hoped we would pass unnoticed. So boldly and straightforwardly, dressed in full British uniform and with our regulation-size packs on our backs, we walked out of the door, turned down the street away from the prison, and a few yards on turned sharply to the right into a small alley. We started to breath again. We were out. We were past the guards. We were free.

As we made our way towards the mental hospital, we knew we had about 15 minutes before curfew. As we turned into the main street, there were more people around, but they were all hurrying home and they didn't take any notice of us. Ten minutes had passed, and I began to wonder if I had remembered the way correctly. Would we find ourselves wandering around a hostile city full of troops who had orders to shoot anyone on the street after curfew? We walked on, and then suddenly the street widened, and there was the little square with the mental hospital over on the far corner.

We crossed over and knocked on the door. It was opened by one of the nuns whom I had met three days previously. I said, in my rather halting Italian, 'You remember me?' 'Yes,' she said and then suddenly, 'But what are you doing here?' When I said, 'We've escaped,' she clapped her hands with delight and took us inside to meet the other sisters and eventually the Mother Superior. After hearing our story, there was a hurried consultation and then we were taken into a guest room and slept peacefully and well.

Next morning, the medical superintendent came along, and in a mixture of French and Italian he told us he was sorry he couldn't keep us there until the Allies came, but that he would find us clothes and a guide up the mountains.

So it was all agreed, and after eating the best meal we had had in months, two delightful Franciscans came to our room. We put on the funny serge hospital suits they had brought us and packed up our belongings, and the food we had saved, into brown paper parcels. Towards dusk we left the hospital, and one of the Franciscans guided us across the town – he walking on the other side of the road – towards the railway station. Up and down the streets we passed, through which walked German soldiers, as well as Italian civilians. They were just enjoying their leisure in the early evening – and we rather enjoyed it, too, being so near to them and being unrecognized.

Ten years later I was in Italy and went to Piacenza to see if I could find this mental hospital again. I knocked at the door as I had done ten years previously. A sister opened it, and I said my piece about having been helped by them in 1943. She looked at me with great delight and said,

19

and I opened the door to you on that occasion!', and then she took me in. The Mother Superior came and with equal exuberance said, 'We thought of you. We said mass for you. We are so thankful you survived,' and then added, 'I hope you haven't told anybody what we did, as it was against all our regulations.'

At the time we didn't know how much hue and cry would have been started for us – but we did know our friends planned to hide the fact of our escape for at least 24 hours. Later we learned that they had in fact kept it secret for more than two days.

As we approached the railway station, the other Franciscan came up behind us and quickly gave us rail tickets for the little mountain railway. We went towards the entrance, and as our guide waited by the platform entrance, we waited also. A moment later, four German Luftwaffe men came and stood a couple of yards from us, and there was an embarrassing moment when an Italian came up to Fred, who was smoking a cigarette, and asked him for one. Fortunately, Fred had learned to shrug his shoulders like an Italian, so he didn't need to say anything, which was lucky as his Italian consisted of just two or three words. The boy moved away without the Germans suspecting anything. Our Italian friends had assured us that the Germans never used this mountain railway.

Then the train came in. Our Franciscan friend walked through the barrier and up to the first coach. We followed and got in the same coach, some seats away from him. Then in walked the four German Luftwaffe, and off we all went into the mountains together. I pretended to doze off – but when a few stations along the line the Germans got off, a certain half smile in our direction from one of the Italians in the coach made me think that our disguise was not very convincing.

A few stops further on, the Italian sitting next to me asked, *'Dove siamo?'* ('Where are we?'), to which I replied with a mumbled, *'Non lo so'* ('I don't know'). To my delight he seemed quite unsuspecting – and so more at ease we dozed on as the train took us up to the end of the line. It was very dark as we walked out of the station at the little mountain town of Bettola with the few other passengers who had come out of the city to their homes in the mountains.

We followed our Franciscan guide as he made his way out of the town towards a bridge over the river – and inside me it seemed as if:

20

Everyone suddenly burst out singing
And I was filled with such delight
As prisoned birds must find in freedom
Winging wildly across the white
Orchards and dark green fields – on; on
And out of sight.

Walking through Bettola with
friends some years later

Chapter 3   THE MOUNTAINS

THERE was a crisp feel of mountain air, the sound of running water, a rough road under our feet, and around us a glorious, although largely unseen, expanse of mountain, forest and of sky. It felt like my own beloved Lakeland country. I remember murmuring to myself, 'Mountains, mountains, glorious mountains.' We were free. We could wander up this road, go as far as we liked. No more barbed wire, no more sentries, no more weary roll calls three times a day. For the first time in 18 months we didn't know exactly what tomorrow would be like. Our Franciscan friend left us with his blessing and the advice to get off the track as soon as possible.

We stopped and unwrapped our parcels and arranged the contents in a more easily portable fashion and then, almost jauntily, stepped out along the road.

Soon we left the houses behind and when we came to a solitary house we stopped to ask for a place to sleep but as there was no answer to our knocking we went on and at the first opportunity turned off the road. The muddy path we took wound up and up through thick trees until we almost despaired of finding a house and were somewhat dismayed at the thought of spending our first night sleeping in the woods.

Eventually we saw a light in the distance and after a few more minutes climb we found ourselves outside a biggish farmhouse. At one side there was a light burning so I knocked at the little side door. It was opened by a young boy of about 15 years of age, and I said my piece, 'We are escaped prisoners of war. Have you a place where we can sleep the night?' He seemed to understand and went back into the room and brought an older chap. I again said my piece and he invited us into a small kitchen where there were several young people, three or four girls and two or three young fellows. We dragged our baggage in and thankfully sat down. The girls appeared very friendly and excited at having two English men with them. One of the fellows was friendly but the other seemed a bit frightened. They said they would have to ask the *padrone* (master) if

23

we could sleep there and one of them went off to call him. Shortly afterwards he appeared in his pyjamas and again I told him who we were. He asked us if we were going on in the morning and when I replied in the affirmative he said it would be all right, and gave instructions to one of the fellows. He appeared an intelligent man, middle-aged, a gentleman farmer type.

Conversation was difficult and after asking me if I spoke French, to which I replied a little but worse than Italian, he returned to bed. One of the girls asked if we were tired and wished to go to bed. I replied that as this was the first time I had talked to a *signorina* for two years I didn't want it to end so soon, and they seemed to enjoy the compliment. We opened our packs and made some cocoa and gave them all some chocolate – a thing they had not seen for three years or more. They struck me as being country folk but very much in touch with the life of the cities. Two of the men were from Rome. They had escaped at the time of the Armistice and were living at the farm.

That night I slept for the first time in my life in a barn. It was warm, fairly comfortable, but there was a wretched rat or mouse that kept running about which was disturbing. However I slept fairly soundly all the same and we got up late the next morning. We were wakened by the young boy of the farm who had promised to guide us up the valley in the direction of several small villages, where some English were supposed to be staying.

We washed at the pump, the water from which flowed into two or three cow troughs and was used for every purpose. While we were washing the woman from the cottage near the farm asked us if we were hungry and insisted that we went into her cottage to have something to eat. We went up a flight of stairs to the living room, which was a bare long room lighted by a small window at the far end. A fire was burning half heartedly in the grate, and an old woman was sitting beside it smoking. There was a man by the window mending shoes who greeted us and, to show that we were welcome, told us to sit down. The first thing that struck me after the bareness was the incredible number of flies. They crawled over the table, over the ceiling, over the floor and where there was the slightest trace of food they resembled a rugby scrum.

Presently the woman brought us two steaming hot bowls of milk with sugar and bread. I thought for a moment of the flies and all the things I knew about infected milk, but I was hungry and it looked very good. We

24

Visiting with friends, the first family to shelter the author – ten years later

were going to drink the milk and eat the bread separately, but they insisted that we break the bread into the milk and eat it like the bread and milk we sometimes had at home when we were ill. They put plenty of sugar in and it tasted very good. The woman never seemed to stop working, and her little girl, who seemed rather sullen and perhaps frightened, refused to smile at us and like her mother went on working. I had never seen people who seemed so poor as this before and had so little food to share, but when we stopped eating to take our breath they would encourage us with '*mangi, mangi*'. When we had finished the milk they brought us some cheese to eat with the bread and insisted on our eating until we could eat no more.

We found the cheese in these mountain villages very good. The only trouble was that it was unwise to look at it as it was swarming with maggots. We gathered that this kind with maggots sold for a higher price than that without.

A few minutes later the young boy from the farm re-appeared to guide us on our way. He had promised to accompany us for a part of the journey until we could see the village where some of our people were supposed to be living. We loaded ourselves with our kit, the boy insisting on carrying a part, and we started to climb up the hillside. The valley and the small town of Bettola we had left the previous night were hidden in a ground mist, but the hills stood out with an almost transparent clarity in the bright morning air. The hills were wooded, and the trees had only just started to turn. We could see something of the shape of the valley through which the river ran, where it was not covered in mist.

25

As we climbed the perspiration rolled from us. We had spent the last month in bed for the most part and with the minimum of exercise, and the hills were steep and the packs rather heavy. The rough path wound up and up through trees and short scrub. Here and there we would pass an open space on the hillside, where a peasant working in the fields would stop and stare at us and ask the boy who we were. As we got higher we saw several small flocks of sheep accompanied by children, for the most part very young ones. They stared at us and no wonder.

Although our disguise had proved adequate for the railway journey in a badly lit train, here in the open hillside it was rather different. We had black trousers, far too short in the leg, an almost black jacket with a khaki shirt and a British service pack, with two British greatcoats half concealed in brown paper. Our get up was sufficient to make any peasant stare, but it mattered little for all seemed friendly.

We reached the brow of the hill from where we could see several groups of buildings, which we took to be

Showing friends the route he took – ten years later

farms. The boy pointed out to us one group that lay three or four miles away and told us that the path we were on would lead us there and that he must now get back to his work. We thanked him and started along the track, but it was not long before it divided and we chose the one that seemed to go in the right direction. Soon it divided again and then it dwindled down to little more than a sheep track. We, of course, concluded that we had taken the wrong path. But later we discovered that these footpaths generally start from a village and extend for about a mile

26

and are reasonably clear, but from then on until you get within about a mile of the next village you are left to your own devices. You are lucky if you hit the path that runs to the village you want to arrive at. The other footpaths all lead into the woods, where wood is cut, or into the fields.

However, it was not long before we found ourselves walking through fields, and so we ceased to worry about paths and made our way in the direction of a farm. We stopped frequently, for we tired quickly; but for all that we went light-heartedly and enjoyed every minute of the journey drinking in the wonder of the mountain scenery. It was about midday when we reached what we had thought to be a farm.

It proved to be a collection of houses with a smallish church in the centre. I had got the idea that every group of houses would be one farm with one master and a number of workmen, so on entering the village I asked for the *padrone*, thinking that there we would probably receive the best treatment. The oldest man of the three I spoke to said he was the *padrone,* and in response to my enquiry as to whether it would be possible for us to stay there, he answered with the nod of his head. He indicated that we should go along with a shrivelled little woman who had just come down between the houses, over the cobbles and mud which served as a street. We accompanied her and she told us that several of our people had passed through the village.

We approached a row of houses, about six in number, and followed her up a flight of stairs into one of them. This brought us into a bare room, similar to the last one, where there were several rather dirty little children playing. In the corner by the window was a girl of about 19 doing her hair. The woman, after giving us chairs, informed us that this was her daughter. I nodded my head by way of acknowledging the introduction, as I did not know the proper words to say, but she seemed too shy to greet us.

The old lady apologised to us for the dirty state of the house and said how difficult it was with young children to keep things in order.   She started to sweep the rough asphalt floor. Everywhere she went she raised a swarm of flies. Presently the man we had first spoken to came in and the girl prepared the table for *pranzo.* The big copper pot which had been boiling over the open fire, suspended from an iron hook, was taken down and emptied into an enamel dish.

27

We were then invited to the table and our plates were filled with *minestra*, a soup consisting of macaroni and beans. The old man sat at the table with us, but the children and the grown up daughter ate their soup away from the table, while the old lady was half at the table as if it was almost her privilege to sit at the table and eat, but that she was not a full member. As soon as our plates were empty they filled them up with more soup, the old man encouraging us by saying that there would not be much food in the evening. After three plates, when we protested that it was not possible for us to eat more, the mother and the children started to tuck into it, and we were pressed to eat bread and cheese. The cheese, I soon gathered, was precious, as the man took but a thin shaving of it; we followed suit and found it excellent.

Conversation was far from easy, as I had little practice in Italian, but I gathered that they had a son who had been with the Italian army in Greece at the time of the Armistice and of whom they had received no word. I also learned that there were two majors living up in a shepherd's hut who came down to the village every four days for food.

The daughter had by this time lost her shyness and talked away to us. She told us that she had been working in the rice fields during the summer. As Fred had been at a work camp and spent some time in the rice fields too, there was a point of contact that helped break the shyness. There were many things to talk about, questions to ask and answers to be given about the way we lived in England compared with Italy. I soon learnt that in this village, and in most villages for that matter, everyone owned a little piece of land, and a few cows, sheep, pigs and hens, and that there was no large farm or *padrone*.

It was true that in some villages the land was owned by a signor, a *padrone* who usually lived in a city, and the peasants sent him half of their crops and produce by way of rent. In this village they lived almost entirely off the small piece of land they cultivated. They milled their grain at the local mill and from the cows they had milk and cheese.

Fruit they grew near the house and from the tomatoes they grew they made conserve with which they flavoured their food. From the sheep they got wool, and after treating it themselves they spun it in the kitchen and later knitted socks and pullovers and jumpers with it. The remainder of their animals they usually sold and with the lire they received they bought clothes, oil, salt, sugar,

28

kitchen utensils and other things which they did not produce on their own land.

The parcel of food which the nuns at Piacenza had given me contained a big slab of salami. We asked them to have this for the evening meal, otherwise it might go bad. They took a lot of persuading and in return insisted on giving us cheese when we left the following day. We learned that meat to them was the height of luxury and a thing they only had when it was a very special *festa*.

It was that evening we saw *polenta* made for the first time. There was a great copper pot on the fire full of water. When the water was boiling a yellow flour was poured in and stirred all the time with a curved wooden stick. The flour was poured in very slowly, taking nearly half an hour before it was all in, by which time it had thickened into a very solid paste. They continued to stir for some time, scraping the mixture from the side and bottom with a sweep of the curved stick, the mixture bubbling and steaming all the time over the roaring wood fire. When the mixture was almost too solid to move, it was taken off the fire and poured on to a board where it set in a solid mass.

The girl asked if we used *polenta* in England and what we called it. I had never seen anything like it before, and so I looked the word up in my pocket dictionary and found that in English it is either called by the same name, polenta, or quick cake. Later I discovered that it was made from maize. When the *polenta* was set it was cut into slices, like thick bread, by means of a piece of string which was simply pulled down vertically at the side of the heap. We then took the portion which had been cut in our fingers. We were invited to taste it and found it to be a very tasteless mixture, but eaten with cheese for flavouring it was not too bad.

We asked them to brew us some tea and the old man had a cup with us but the rest of the family refused to taste it. They were very suspicious of anything new in the way of food, and tea, except in the cities, seemed to be uncommon.

The mother of the family was, of course, interested in our families and it was not long before they knew our ages, families and where we lived, how long we had been in the army and how long we had been away from home.

She, by the way, could not have been more than 45 to 50 years of age but these Italian mountain women, good looking and often pretty as girls, worked so hard that before they were 40 they looked like someone of 60 or 70. Most of

29

them reared very large families, and a woman's job was to cook, do all the house work, carry the water from the well, feed the hens and pigs that were generally kept on the ground floor of the house, help in the fields when necessary, and at the same time bring into the world and rear a dozen children.

The woman of this house was typical. She was small but seemed capable of a great amount of work. Her clothes were patched beyond recognition, and over her head was draped a black cotton scarf so that her hair was always out of sight. Her face and hands were brown and creased like a piece of old leather, but her watery eyes were kind and sympathetic. Woollen stockings, heavily darned, and on her feet a pair of derelict shoes completed her dress. She was lucky. Most of them wore wooden shoes or at least shoes with wooden soles. Leather had practically disappeared from their world.

After the meal we sat round the fire talking. The room was lit by a very feeble oil lamp. About half-past-eight or nine they asked if we were sleepy and we replied that we were ready for bed. The old man showed us out to the back and into the hay loft over the living room.

I had quite a lot of clothes with me including pyjamas, and I used them all to cover some part of me, and with my great coat over the top, and with the straw pulled well over me, I was very comfortable. The loft ran the whole length of the row of houses and was only divided by a few boards. We heard a noise from over the partition and thought it must be rats, but later decided that it was someone sleeping there, so we soon settled down to a deep sleep after our first day in the mountains.

The next day was misty and dull, with a constant threat of rain. We got up late and after eating our bread and milk we sat about hoping that the weather would clear. The mother and daughter wanted us to stay on for the day, but when the weather seemed to clear a little towards two o'clock we decided to move.

I was as yet without any very clear plan of what to do. My original idea had been to stay at Piacenza, and when that had been impracticable, we had come out into the mountains with only a vague idea of what we would do. At the back of my mind I had the idea of moving down through the mountains towards our troops.

But the first thing was to get fit. For that purpose we had brought the Red Cross food with us and the plan was to walk a little each day, eat good food and get ourselves

30

in trim for a journey. I had only the vaguest idea of what Italy was like beyond knowing that it was shaped like a leg. Although I had occasionally seen a map in the camp and had even copied one, I had really no idea that the Appennine chain ran right down the centre of the country and that the mountains were from over 3,000 to over 8,000 feet in height.

Although we had only been away from the hospital two and a half days, we were very keen to meet some of our own people. We'd been pitched head first into another world, a world of different values, of danger, a larger and more exciting world than our prison world. We felt very lost and insecure. We only understood half of what was said to us. We had little idea of how much danger there was and who we could trust. We'd been put on a train and sent to the mountains; all we knew was that somewhere to the west was Genoa and somewhere to the south-west, Spezia. And so as we went we kept our eyes open in the hope of meeting some of our own people so that we could learn more of what the situation was.

We set off from the village with the idea of following the river up into the higher mountains, that is in a south-west direction, and then going south-east among the higher mountains. We followed a path for a while, passed through another very small village and the path began to divide in the usual manner. The footpath became worse and worse and the mist thickened in all around us. After a while we struck what looked like cart tracks and so I became more hopeful, only to find ourselves in the middle of a wood. We had followed the tracks of the sleighs they use for collecting firewood.

We went on. It started to rain, and before many minutes had gone we found ourselves forcing our way through thick undergrowth. After about a quarter of an hour it got so thick that we could hardly move either forward or backwards. The way was barred by low branches, by creepers, by brambles and by everything prickly all bound together in a tangled mass. e were scratched. Our clothes, which were not of the strongest material, began to tear and rip, and we were very wet as well. I think we were very frightened, lost in a wood, soaking wet, feeling rather weak and completely uncertain about where we were, and wondering whether this whole escape had any possibility of success.

We turned to climb up the hill a bit hoping to strike clearer ground, but after scrambling up rocks we found ourselves in undergrowth which was just as impassable.

We could only see 20 to 30 yards and we rested awhile, breathless, to consider our position. Finally we decided that the only certain way of getting out of the wood was to return back on our own tracks, which we did until we reached the footpath again. Hearing voices we stopped to let the people pass as we had no idea as to who they might be. Then we followed another path and in less than half an hour we found ourselves outside a small village.

We were so thankful to be out of the woods that we knocked at the door of one of the first houses, a large one, and were greeted by a girl. We asked if we might go in and dry ourselves and she showed us into a room where there were several fellows sitting round and we soon realised that this was an *osteria*. I never thought that in a remote village like this one we would find a pub. There was a good fire and after dropping our packs in the corner we went to warm ourselves.

There were two young Italians there who seemed very friendly and told the girls to bring us drinks which were very refreshing. We learnt that they were Italian soldiers on their way up to join a band of rebels who were forming in a village about four hours away. There were Italians and English and they had weapons and ammunition: we must go along with them. We said that just now we were very tired; we would see later.

The girl who had shown us in, came and joined in the conversation and, of course, wanted to know where we had come from, what was the matter with my eye, and all the other questions. She informed us quite casually that there were two British officers staying in this very village. Immediately I asked if we could see them, but she was rather reticent and said that they didn't wish to see anyone. People kept coming in and out of the room and presently we were invited to have some food. By this time we were quite hungry and very glad of the *pastasciuta* that they offered us.

MEETING THE COLONELS

After the meal we went upstairs to listen to the radio and we had only been there a moment when in walked a big, middle-aged, jolly-looking man dressed in black trousers and a polo neck. We introduced ourselves. For us it seemed like the meeting of Livingstone and Stanley in Central Africa. He was an Australian colonel commanding

32

an English battalion of a north country regiment. I had a great friend in his battalion and so we were soon talking like old friends. He suggested that we leave the *osteria* and go with him; a lot of strangers came there, and it was not a good thing for it to get about that they were living there.

We went to the barn where he was living and he invited us to stay with him that night. He apologised for being rather inaccessible. He had told the villagers not to bring people to them, but bring news first, as in their first days there they had brought all sorts of people to see them. He told us there was another officer, Colonel Fanshaw from a cavalry regiment, who, with his batman was living in another barn nearby.

The whole camp in which they had been prisoners (Senior Officers' Camp, near Piacenza) had escaped at the Armistice called between Italy and the Allies. The first fortnight they had spent in the woods, living off the food they had brought with them, as they didn't know whether the Italian people were for or against them. When they were near this village the children with their flocks of sheep had discovered them and had brought them food. Eventually they had come down to the village, and as Colonel Fanshaw had hurt his knee they had decided to stay. One of the villagers had been in America and so they made him their agent, giving him an order on the bank, and each day they went to a different house for supper, *cena*, in the evening.

It was a small village, probably not more than a dozen families. The colonels had a certain amount of food with them that they used during the day. They had made themselves very comfortable and the villagers were all friendly. There was a larger village nearby and every other day Colonel Fanshaw, who was Roman Catholic, went down at dusk to the priest there and listened to his radio.

As we were talking one of the villagers brought news that the local police sergeant was coming up to the village. It seemed he was friendly, but to save him embarrassment they always went up to the fields when he visited the village.

We went out and met Colonel Fanshaw and his batman and made our way up the hill at the back. The barns were situated at the top of the village so that access to the fields and woods behind was very quick. In the fields we met an Italian woman, small, shrivelled and dressed in old black clothes, but to my amazement she started talking to us in English with a broad American accent. She was the wife of the fellow who had been in America. Further up we met her husband busy hoeing a field. The two colonels had been up there the previous day helping him and all the villagers were amazed at them.

Both colonels were six feet two inches and dressed in dyed battle dress, pullovers and old hats, one felt and the other straw. They looked rather remarkable, especially when hoeing a field. I liked the Italian and his wife very much; although they had seen something of the world they were simple, unspoilt and kind. They invited us to join with the other three to dinner at their house that night. Each family took it in turn and that night it was their turn.

The weather had cleared somewhat and we sat down on a bank while Colonel Fanshaw showed me the lie of the valley, where the river and the main road ran, pointing out the two villages which the Germans occasionally visited.

It seemed a different world from that of the morning. We'd been lost in the mist in a strange unknown land and now we were with friends, the sun was shining and we knew where there was danger and where we were comparatively secure.

In the evening we went out to dinner with this family and it was a good one. I have forgotten what we had exactly but I know there was no meat and I remember that we had a chocolate blancmange. It must have been made from packets the two colonels had given them. We also had coffee, imitation but all the same it was good.

They had a daughter of 19, who did all the cooking and most of the housework in spite of a short and malformed leg. She was dark, with the brightest, darkest eyes I had ever seen. Her features were regular, her skin olive, but with lovely rosy cheeks and the sweetest smile imaginable. She had suffered a lot and her father had spent a lot of money on expensive operations, but she seemed very content. After the meal several other young girls came in – the colonels were very popular with them – and we spent the evening talking and teaching them English words and learning Italian ones.

The little hard pears you often find in England they boiled here and ate as a sweet. We ate lots that evening and very good they were too. I think that evening, with the joking and laughter and the company of the two good folks and their children and friends was the happiest I had spent for two or three years. I had never realised before prison life what a difference the company of children and women folk made, but especially children.

34

We learnt many things from the two colonels before we left. They had a good map of the area and I was able to get a fair idea of the lie of the land. We learnt too that in this area doctors who were pro British were carrying a Red Cross on their right headlamp.

I remember too them telling me a story about our friend who had been in America. It appears that he had two lots of land, one in this village and the other near Bettola ten miles away. The man to whom he had let the second plot had been unable to pay his rent, and to meet his liability he had offered to give him one of his children. Our friend had refused because he had enough children to look after his sheep and to help with the work, but I don't think it struck him as being unusual.

We did not leave the following day until after lunch, as the village tailor was mending my trousers for me, but when we did leave it was with a certain amount of sadness, as it seemed we were leaving a village of friends.
The colonels had information that certain villages were friendly, and I had chosen one about two hours away that was in the general direction that I wished to take. The villagers pointed the way out to us and with our huge bundles on our backs we left them behind.

There were many fascinating encounters. One I remember well was with a tall good looking boy of about 15 who was wearing long plus-four trousers and looking after some sheep. He told us his father had been in America and invited us to go and meet him. The boy, asking us about our escape, was delighted to learn that the prison hospital we'd escaped from was in the very school building where he'd been educated in peacetime.

Later that day we were welcomed by his father and mother who, although quite well off now, were very typical mountain folk. Their own daughters and son were obviously being well educated and looked very smart but also were delighted in their mamma and papa. That night I heard an English radio programme for the first time in two years. I was quite excited to hear simply the words, 'This is the BBC'.

We decided to rest in that area for two or three days. The weather was dull. We were in the clouds. It was hard to realise that we were living between 2,000 and 3,000 feet above sea level, as we had done no really stiff climbs but just gone a little higher each day.

The sense of freedom which I had can best be described by comparing it with the disappearance of a toothache or a

35

bodily pain or illness. At the camp, even when I was really fit, I always felt as if one of my faculties was missing or out of order. Now, even though I had in fact lost the use of one eye, I felt whole again.

The colonels had advised us to stop in this area, as they considered that to walk to the south was nearly impossible; boots would wear out, snow would come before we got there, and the line would be too difficult to cross. They also considered there would probably be a landing in the north before long. My reasoning was rather different. I considered that for any landing that was made the further south we were the better it would be. Therefore as long as we were fit, and the weather was good, it was better to walk, and if our boots showed signs of wearing out we could find a place to stop.

I considered that the danger in travelling was not much greater than that of staying in one place, as in the latter case it became well known and there was always the possibility of a spy informing the Germans, and of them sending a patrol. Added to this was the fact that it was necessary to find people who were willing to keep us for a considerable time.

As yet we'd had no difficulty regarding food. People had given us a good dinner each night and others had given us food for the day. The barns we were sleeping in at the moment were hay barns and not very comfortable. I also thought, and experience proved me right, that when you passed through several villages every day and slept at a different one each night, food was easier to find and generally better. The peasants simply had not enough to spare to give constantly, but when it was just for one night or one meal that we stopped they produced the best they could.

However, I rather gathered that Fred liked the idea of staying. We'd made good friends, there was lots of *vino* and quite a social life.

I felt that at this point there were really three alternatives. Firstly, to take the colonels' advice, secondly, to make for Switzerland 100 miles to the north, or thirdly, to go south hoping to join the Allies who had landed in Calabria, and who we believed would advance rapidly up the country.

Once again I searched in my heart for the leading of the Holy Spirit and rather to my surprise came the clear thought, 'Go south'. There were good reasons for this decision but the leading of the Holy Spirit was like the starting

36

gun in a race. It made you go. Later it became clear that this was the right decision. Those who went to Switzerland were interned for three years, and most of those who stayed in the villages were recaptured.

So we decided that the time had come to start our trek to the south. By now we had walked quite a bit, and our legs had lost their stiffness. We had eaten good food, more food than we had been used to during the previous two years, and our bodies were beginning to recover from the long months on short rations. We had lightened our packs and were getting used to carrying them. We believed at the time that, as the Allies would advance quickly, we would meet them halfway. In fact we had to walk some 700 miles before we reached the fighting line.

Chapter 4   THE TREK TO THE SOUTH

ON the ninth day after our escape, the 12th October, we seriously started our trek. It was no longer in a holiday spirit that we went, but with a simple determination to reach the Allies. The mist of the previous days, which had made us feel that it was almost winter, had disappeared, and the sun was shining. Although we'd had some directions from our friends, we soon lost our way and had to retrace our steps several times in order to reach a bridge over the river. It was a long way down, and then we realised just how high in the mountains were the villages we'd been staying in. These lower villages seemed to us dangerous, but we discovered that the Germans passed up the roads only occasionally and seldom left their trucks or explored either the mule tracks or the villages to which they led.

As we came to the road along the valley, we watched the bridge. One civilian car passed, but as nothing else was in sight, we jumped down on to the road, and with a certain nervousness crossed the bridge which was about 50 yards long. Our fear was that a German army vehicle would suddenly come round the corner of the road – less than a mile away – and catch us there in the middle of the bridge. All was well.

We were to have this experience of crossing a road or a bridge scores of times in the next months, and the further south we got and the nearer to the fighting the more dangerous it became.

The first few days were amongst the most difficult. The relationship between Fred and myself was a difficult one to work out. I was an officer, and he a guardsman, and although I'd made it clear to him that this didn't count now and we were in this together, he found it difficult to accept and also to say what he thought.

The first day after crossing that first bridge we had to make one of the steepest rock climbs of the journey. I enjoyed it, but Fred didn't like heights and although a countryman he was not keen on climbing. The day ended with us finding a rather unfriendly and frightened village. Eventually we were offered benches to sleep on in the

39

living room of a family. But very early in the morning, before first light, the man of the house came to us. He was very excited and nervous and told us we must go immediately: the Germans were nearby, they had surrounded the next village and taken away the priest and two prisoners whom he was harbouring. So we had to leave, without the usual milk and bread and not in the best of tempers, and then climb as quickly as we could out of the valley. We did a lot this day. We had to wade across a stream to move swiftly from the nearest villages because the Germans had done a quick circuit of them looking for escaped prisoners. So we had to circle a mountain because the villages in the valley were too large and therefore dangerous for us. In 12 hours' walking that day, we reckoned we'd covered about seven miles of our route.

It was really no wonder that Fred became disgruntled. He then said he thought we'd been wrong not to accept the two colonels' advice and settle down, as it was really crazy to tackle the hundreds of miles of mountains to the south without map or compass. I told him he could have stayed, but at the same time I realised that for me to go on alone, barely having got used to seeing with one eye, would have been perilous indeed.

Gradually we worked through this, partly because we were constantly receiving word of escaped prisoners being recaptured, and also because it was clear that the Allies were not advancing quickly at all and that we might have waited there for a year or more before our troops came. Also we got to know each other and eventually a real friendship developed.

I have wondered since whether I should have told Fred the basis of my decision to go south. At that time I was rather shy about talking of my faith. I don't really know whether it would have given him more confidence or not.

*   *   *   *   *

As we journeyed southwards, it wasn't always that I got very clear thoughts of what to do – although sometimes I had a compelling sense to take one road or another. Generally it was a certain inner prompting which led me to choose the higher routes, the more difficult paths, and bred in me a knowledge of the best ways to get over these rugged mountains. We were led, I felt, to stay out of the dangerous valleys and up on the lonely slopes where sometimes we wouldn't see a single human being during a whole day. I think that it was God training me to live on those mountains, rather than telling me all the time what to do – although the general direction and line we should pursue were generally made plain.

Soon we came into chestnut country. In the evenings we would often sit round a fire helping a family to peel the chestnuts and at the same time eating large quantities of them. You were expected to eat 40 or 50 an evening – but it took us a little time to reach that level. One night when we had nowhere else to go, we slept on the floor of the roasting hut, a round brick building with a constant wood fire in the centre and slats above which the chestnuts were being roasted, and then eventually sold in the cities for high prices. By getting down flat on the floor we avoided getting too smoked ourselves. It was warm, but not to be recommended.

By this time we were getting used to the habits and practices of the mountain folk. We knew that if we wanted a drink of water we went to one of the buckets and drank out of the big copper ladle. We learnt not to look surprised if the man or even the woman of the house spat into the fire or on to the floor. They nearly always put a table cloth on the table for us, although in many houses we could see that it was not the usual practice. The plates, cutlery and cooking pots always seemed to be kept clean. One night we slept for the first time with the cows, and we discovered that from the point of view of warmth it couldn't be beaten. The only trouble with the cowshed was that all the cows had bells round their necks and so for the first two or three hours, and intermittently through the night, our rest was accompanied by the jingle of bells. Our bed that night was of dry leaves and the only disadvantage was that among them were some of the prickly outer coverings of chestnuts. If you happened to lie on one you knew about it pretty quickly.

I was gradually becoming a connoisseur of barns, and one of the undesirable features I discovered was hay. Firstly it was not as warm as straw, secondly it was dirty and thirdly it crept in your clothes, sticking to everything, tickling your skin all day and taking about a half hour each morning to get rid of the worst of it.

In these early days of our trek we met a school master who gave us a motoring map of Italy. This was a very great help. Although it didn't mark any of the mule tracks, we knew that any village that was marked on the map and so had a road running through it, was to be avoided. It also gave us a general idea of the direction to take and the height of the mountains. It showed us clearly that the Appennine ridge ran right down the Italian peninsula with the roads intersecting the mountains going through high passes. Clearly our best plan was to keep to the high ground. *(See map reproduced opposite.)*

One day we heard of a British general in the area who, it was said, had a radio transmitter. We were told to contact him through a priest. Although it meant turning back on our tracks we thought it was worth looking into.

When we reached the village indicated we found the priest was away, so we spent the day by a stream, getting a good wash ourselves and also washing our clothes which were badly in need of it. I think some of the older mountain folk thought that to wash in a mountain stream in October was overdoing it.

Eventually the priest arrived. He was rather frightened and said he knew nothing about this general. He advised us to live in the mountains and not to come down to the villages. Whilst we were talking a middle aged fellow came in. He'd lived in Wales for a long time. He was very friendly and talked English exactly like a Welshman. We discovered that in that valley a lot of them had been in Wales, and the following day, having walked very little owing to a thick mist, we found ourselves with a family who seemed very British. All three of them, mother, father and daughter, spoke English perfectly. The daughter had been brought up in Britain. They had an ice cream business near Cardiff and had been caught in Italy when war broke out. It was almost like being in a British home again and with British people. They cooked by electricity; they gave us English food and knew exactly what we were used to. It was delightful.

We could see, however, that the father was frightened. When we first arrived asking for a place for the night he had replied that he hadn't one, and so we had left the village (only about ten houses) but he ran after us and asked us if we would come and have something to eat and he would find us a place to sleep, which he did.

The following morning, in spite of the persistent mist, we left early and decided to stop at the first really friendly village. We were beginning to think that the friendliness of the first few villages near Bettola was exceptional and that this atmosphere of fear was the most usual thing to expect. We passed through two villages whose people were friendly but frightened, and it was fortunate that we

Motoring map used by the author during his escape. The dotted line shows the route he took.

did not stay at either as later in the day the Germans came to these villages, dressed in civilian clothes, saying they were escaped English prisoners and asking for food and lodging. We heard that they had taken the young men from the house that gave them food.

We then climbed out of the valley and up the mountainside in thick mist until we reached a charcoal burner's hut. It was a ramshackle hut, an hour's climb from the nearest village, in a dense wood nearly at the top of a mountain. We found there a family of half a dozen children with their father and mother. It was like coming into another world. For all their dirt and squalor they were kind folk, sorry not to be able to give us food, but as they explained they grew no food of their own and had to buy all they needed, and that was extremely difficult at that time. These people called *carbonari* lived mainly in whole families, high in the mountain forests. They would build a shack to live in and then turn smouldering piles of wood into charcoal, which is a major fuel in the cities. They were black from head to foot, looking rather like the chimney sweeps of my youth. They spent many months up in the forest cutting the wood, tending the fires, and then carting the charcoal down to the nearest village. If there were many of them working together they would rig up a *fumeria*, buckets suspended on wires and worked by a series of pulleys, taking the charcoal from high up to the road below.

They directed us to a valley to the left, as it was too risky in the thick fog to go over the top of the mountain in our proper direction. As we reached the valley the mist began to clear, and we were able to see half a dozen villages nestling round the basin-like valley. We approached the nearest one. We were refused help in one house but then invited into another house by a young man. It was our practice never to ask for food, always just for a night's lodging, but these kind hearted people never failed to give us food, often the very food they were going to eat themselves.

I could see that these people were rather worried and after a while the husband went out and brought back with him a middle aged man who spoke nearly perfect English. He interrogated us as to where we came from, and when Fred said near London he said, 'But you're not a cockney,' and Fred explained that he was born in Northumberland. He nodded to the young couple as if to say it's all right, and then turned to us and apologised for the interrogation,

44

but explained that these people were afraid that we were Germans pretending to be English in order to find out which villages were giving help to prisoners, and maybe also to discover by this method whether prisoners were hiding in the area. This English speaking man was some kind of merchant who had spent a lot of time in all parts of England. He advised us to go into Tuscany and told us that the people there were often very fair skinned, the reason being that when Caesar was in Britain he used troops from that part and a lot of them took English wives. He said they were friendly and intelligent, and we came to regard Tuscany as almost the promised land. This family proved to be very helpful to us, and we got our boots studded there.

The following morning a young fellow accompanied us a good way on our journey and gave us directions on which way to go. But we found ourselves rather too near a large village, almost a small town, and so changed direction. We had already walked three hours when we met two young men who were obviously going in the same direction as we were. We were slightly suspicious of them, particularly as one of them was wearing a black tab on his suit. Everything black we associated with the Fascists and everything Fascist was suspect. However, we talked with them for a while and discovered that they were police who, not wishing to serve under the Fascist government, were making their way home. Their village was exactly in our direction and so they invited us to come with them saying we could stay the night there and then they would put us on the right track the following day.

It was a long climb without tracks or sight of villages and certainly on our own it would have taken us a whole day's walking, but with them it took only four or five hours. We arrived at a little village overlooking a larger village and a railway line. The father of the policeman we stayed with had been in America and was very pleased to see us. Like so many Italians who had been in America he had learnt to drink too freely and gave us the impression of being rather drunk. They were a kind family. Already they had two Italian soldiers from Naples living with them who were unable to reach their homes. They gave us the best food they could and as we were hungry we took full advantage of it. We slept that night on two forms in the kitchen and in spite of their hardness slept well.

We were unable to cross the river and railway directly below as there was a large village and a railway station with the German army permanently there. Apparently this platoon was composed of Austrians and like most of the Austrians not very keen on the war, so they disturbed the villagers very little. The real trouble was that there were Fascists working on the railway, and so our policeman friend guided us along the hillside until we reached a long railway bridge. He went down first and enquired from the signalman if there were any Fascists about and finding everything clear, signalled us to come down. The bridge was over a 100 yards long and at the other side passed the provincial road, so that with every step we took our hearts beat faster, afraid that a German car might come round the bend of the road and catch us in the middle of the bridge. However we crossed in safety and bidding farewell to our friend began the climb up the opposite mountain.

A rainstorm forced us to shelter in a friendly farm for most of the day and in the evening we climbed up to the loneliest and strangest farm we ever stayed in. It was situated right on the shoulder of the mountain, open to the wind and rain, a long low building surrounded by woods and rough pasture land. The people asked us in and made us warm ourselves and gave us food and lodging for the night, but there wasn't the usual friendly chatter and questioning. They were silent, almost sullen, and it seemed that some great shadow was hanging over them. Of course we never knew what it was.

Ours was a strange life. In the evenings we would become part of a family scene, each different from the previous one. The daytime was always spent in different country, but very often consisted of climbing up over the shoulder of a mountain at least once in the day. I always found this stimulating. You would be sweating up a steep slope and eventually get towards the top, and then would come into view the whole panorama of the next valley and mountain, and so much would depend on what that scene was like. We generally stopped on the top to eat the bread and cheese which the villagers had so generously provided. Then, with the help of our motoring map, we would pick out the villages to avoid, look for places to cross the valley and make our way towards the lonely mountain hamlets on the other side of the valley. Towards three or four o'clock each day we would begin to think about the night, always with a slight fear that we wouldn't find anywhere to sleep.

As we got accustomed to the pattern, and as we found

that we nearly always encountered friends and a place to sleep, we began to feel a carefreeness as if we were on a walking holiday, with no fixed destination but with a list of villages from the family we'd stayed with the previous night, to guide us in the right direction.

I have a vivid memory of one day when it poured with rain all morning as we climbed up a mule track going over a pass. By the time we got to the top we were soaking wet with the rain, and soaking also inside with sweat. As the rain cleared and a wind got up we went down the mountainside, and to our surprise and delight, by the time we got to the valley we were completely dry again.

The food varied in different parts, but all the mountain folk were generous. The way they ate *polenta* here was different from the north. It was quite an experience. The Indian corn was boiled up on the fire and then poured on to a large pastry board on top of the kitchen table. Then it was rolled out so it was about a quarter to a third of an inch thick and sprinkled with a little tomato conserve and cheese. Then we sat round the table and were given a fork and each of us worked our way towards the centre, with cries of '*mangi, mangi*, eat up,' because we were slower than the rest of the family.

On one part of the journey we found that the people had run out of salt. They usually got it from the south which was now separated from the north by the fighting. We realised, for the first time, just how horrible food tasted without any salt.

It was two days after we had left the strange house on the hill that we had perhaps the most terrifying experience of our journey. At three o'clock in the afternoon we found ourselves in a rather frightened valley. The Germans had been round that day searching for prisoners and escaped Italian soldiers, and even though they were only a handful, they were enough to put fear into the hearts of the villagers for miles around. In front of us was a long high mountain and we were told that half way up, concealed in a hidden valley, were two villages. (In my diary I called one of them 'G' and I have no idea now what it stood for.) The reports as to how long it would take us to walk varied from one to three hours, and when in the late afternoon a low cloud covered the mountainside Fred was for finding a place in the valley for the night. I thought this would be too difficult and dangerous in the present circumstances as most of the villages were very near the provincial road. So after some discussion we decided to make for 'G'. It was not long before we climbed up into the mist. A man we had met at the beginning of the climb told us to keep taking the track to the right past an observation post. After climbing a bit more, he said we would find the hidden valley just below us.

However we soon realised we had lost our way. Presently we heard the sound of cattle and people above us and scrambled up a steep grassy bank until we met up with a man and two women with a number of cattle. They gave us directions and said it shouldn't take us more than three quarters of an hour to reach 'G'. Soon we did reach two empty barracks which we took to be the observation post. We met a man and a boy there who pointed us to a track running round the mountainside which they said would lead us to 'G'. Fred swore that they themselves were going to 'G' and, not wanting us in their village, had deliberately directed us in the wrong direction.

We went on round this track for an hour or more and nowhere was there any path leading down into the valley. All around was thick forest and every minute the mist became thicker and damper. I began to realise that we might have to spend the night there in this dense forest high up in the mountains: it was a frightening thought.

Eventually, because our track was just going on and on at the same level, we decided to turn back and go down one of the waterways even if it took us back to the frightened valley.

Presently we heard voices below us. It took us about 20 minutes of quick scrambling down the mountainside before we caught up with four men and several mules pulling huge sleighs full of wood down the slope. You have no idea how grateful we were to see them and almost light-heartedly we asked them if we would be able to find a place to sleep in their village. Their reply was a complete negative.

They made a big story of Germans all round and were obviously very afraid. We asked them what their village was called and where 'G' was or the other village up the mountain. They pointed back in the direction from which we had come. It was nearly dark and the mist had turned into fine rain, like a scotch mist. I pointed out rather desperately that we had been searching for the village for several hours and it seemed to me that we had less chance of finding it in the dark. I asked if it would be possible for one of them to accompany us for part of the way, but they just looked at each other, shrugged their shoulders, and

48

excused themselves: they must accompany their mules and wood piles.

I took this as a challenge. We didn't want any unwilling hospitality; we would find 'G' in spite of the mist and rain and the dark or we'd stay out in the woods. We turned back and started climbing as fast and as hard as we could. The rain soaked into our clothes and perspiration soaked our underclothes and even our shirts. And then we found ourselves back at the observation post. On top of the hill about 200 yards up a very steep bank we could dimly see another hut. I decided to go along the ridge beside the hut and if I thought that the village lay on the other side I would call to Fred to join me; otherwise I would return and we would spend the night in the hut. It would be better there than completely in the open, although it would have been terrible to pass a night in a hut without windows or doors and little chance of making a fire. Added to this we were soaked, hungry and thirsty, and although we had some food with us there was no water near.

I reached the top and followed one path for a short distance but soon decided it was only the track that ran alongside the telegraph wire, and would take us into the next valley after about four or five hours. I stopped on the ridge and listened, and I felt more than heard the sound of a village down in the valley below and the sound of a dog barking. I signalled to Fred to join me and he came up thankfully, as the idea of a night in the hut pleased him less the longer he stayed there. We could now hear nothing from below. It must have been a fortunate puff of wind that brought that sound to me, but all the same we started to scramble down the mountainside.

We got into a waterway and by following this down we felt sure we would join a track. It was dark now and we ran down over the loose stones and running water, heedless of the risk of a sprained or broken ankle. Down, down we ran, recklessly, and it was with very great relief that we saw the woods thin out around us and the water course take on the semblance of a track. Soon it broadened out into a proper mountain track, a track of loose stones and running water and we hurtled down that with rather less pain to our ankles. After about half an hour of this breathless running and scrambling we came across signs of habitation, fenced fields, hay stacks and firmer roadways. Another ten minutes and we found ourselves outside a little village; sure enough, it proved to be 'G'.

The day's nightmare was over. The first person we met

told us that there was another Englishman there and led us to the house where he was staying. He turned out to be a lieutenant from a camp near Piacenza. Soon we were changing our clothes by a roaring fire – putting on what dry clothes we could from our packs – and enjoying the lovely hospitality of a friendly village. I never remember a fire so bright and cheerful as that one. When we learnt that a week previously two Italian soldiers endeavouring to reach their homes on the other side of the mountain had died of exposure on that same mountain, we were even more thankful. After supper we went to bed and the three of us slept together on the floor of a barn in company with several rabbits. We slept well. The next morning we got up late. There was a strong rumour around that English troops had landed at Livorno. If this was true it meant an alteration to our plans, so we delayed our departure in order to hear the wireless at the local *osteria*; but it was only another rumour, one of the many hundreds we heard on the way.

Then we had three days of gloriously sunny weather and made good distances each day. I wrote in my diary, 'The mountains were high in this area, the highest we have come across, and the view was beautiful and always changing. We climbed over the shoulder of one grass-topped giant, up to a height of between 5 - 6,000 feet, and from there we could see the Appennine range stretched out in front of us. Here and there jutting into the blue Mediterranean sky were the rocky-topped peaks with their bases in thick forests. Down in the valleys and on the sloping sides we could see little specks clustered together surrounded by patches of green and brown. These we knew to be villages surrounded by their cultivated land. It was an enchanting sight and seemed far from the war.' Many times when we were amongst the golds and reds and browns of the autumn trees, I longed to have my paints with me.

At one stage we found ourselves walking over the mountains near to the Fontanellato camp that I'd been in. It was not surprising that one day we met up with two fellows I'd known in the camp. I was delighted to have confirmation that at the Armistice they'd all been allowed to leave by the Italian commandant who was friendly towards the Allies. Many were roaming around this area.

A few days later we were offered a bed in the house of a young couple on a little hill above a small village. Having slept in barns, hay lofts, hard benches, stables, it was ecstasy to sleep in sheets again. A thick mist came down the next day and lasted for six days, so we decided to accept their pressing invitation to stay.

I was also able to find a cobbler in the village below, and after I'd offered him a pound note, he 'discovered' that he had a piece of leather and could put new soles on my boots (which were thin) and sew up the uppers which were coming apart. He did a wonderful job with them.

I wrote in my diary: 'It was November 1st when we left this comfortable spot, with great protests from the young couple as they wanted us to stay. The sun was shining with the warmth and brilliance of an English summer day. There wasn't a cloud in the sky and not a breath of wind disturbed the small lake below the village which reflected the blues and browns of the opposite hills with a wonderful clarity, transforming the colour in the reflection to unbelievable tints, and forming a contrast to the reflected blue of the sky in the nearest part of the water. The trees were beginning to turn to shades of brown and gold. But the heat seemed to give off energy rather than absorb it.'

Our first objective had been to get beyond the Bologna-Florence railway line. We hoped, when that far down the leg of Italy, to get news of our troop movements and to decide whether to make for the east coast or the west.

That first day out from our rest we travelled faster and with greater assurance than ever before, for now we were fit, and we had the map.

The next day there was a thick mist, and after crossing a road we climbed up and eventually over the shoulder of Mount Cimone. When we got above the mist we experienced that wonderful feeling of being above the clouds and watching them as they swirled around the valleys.

We were now among the high mountains, and I described in my diary one incident when we were on top of a steep ridge, and had started to make our way down a very steep slope. We had dropped only 200 or 300 feet when we heard the voice of a child calling us from the left hand cliff above us and a quarter of a mile away. In the clear mountain air sound carries quite easily, and so even at that distance we were able to carry on a conversation. She warned us there was no way down in the direction we were going, but to the left there was a path. So we climbed up to where she was. She was a little girl of not more than ten years of age. We asked her if she was all alone, and she said she was. Every day she came up from her home lower in the valley, loosed the sheep and cattle from their

51

sheds and watched them all day whilst they grazed on the grassy-topped ridge.

In the evening she locked them up again and went home. She was a sweet child with a clear musical voice and spoke the lovely Italian language with beauty and simplicity. She told us many British and Yugoslavs had passed that way. We were quite sorry to leave such a delightful person, and as we made our way down the path she indicated, her voice followed us singing and whistling right down the mountainside.

Our main concern now was to cover a good distance each day, but because of the terrain we were lucky if we did ten miles after eight hours of walking. This was perhaps the most difficult part of the journey. We had been walking for four weeks and had only gone about 150 miles as the crow flies. We weren't crows and had walked about three times that distance. Also we knew that soon the snow would come, and it would be much more difficult to keep to the high mountains. The Allied troops had not advanced, and so we had only covered less than a third of the way to the fighting line. It seemed like an almost impossible dream that we would actually succeed in getting to the line. However, at this point both Fred and myself felt impelled to go on and tackle the impossible.

The weather was good and held out until we crossed the main line railway from Bologna to Florence. We crossed it where there was a very long tunnel through the mountains, so that presented no difficulty.

The next night we had a warm welcome in a lonely farm house. We needed it, as we were soaking wet. When we woke in the morning there was a foot of snow on the ground. Two of the boys from the family guided us down to the nearest village. It was a good job we had these guides as there was no indication of a track, and the drifts of snow concealed dangerous places. Despite this, we enjoyed moving down across the fields, and with the conifers heavily weighted with snow, it was indeed beautiful.

We then crossed the main Bologna-Prato road quite easily – it was well wooded on both sides – and arrived in a prosperous valley rich in olive and fruit trees and vines. We thought that in this rich valley there would be plenty of food. However, the people were frightened, and it was difficult to find a place to sleep. Eventually we were allowed to sleep in a draughty barn, but the next morning we set off with only a handful of chestnuts for breakfast.

The going now consisted of innumerable little valleys. Fortifications, the so-called Gothic line, were being built, and the Germans seemed to be everywhere. This was Tuscany and not quite the dream place we'd envisaged. Also the Tuscan accent, although delightful, was at first more difficult to understand.

This was, I think, our worst day, possibly because we had had no breakfast. It was pouring with rain, and everyone was afraid. In the end all was well. We met a man who seemed rather frightened to begin with, but who gave us a good dinner and found us a bed for the night with a family who kept what they called the English room, as a number of escaped prisoners had passed this way.

Their son accompanied us for two hours the next morning and then gave us directions for the next day or so. Once more we found ourselves in the mountains and there was a friendly atmosphere again and more food. It was easier to find our way.

We had a narrow escape, however, whilst crossing what we thought was a secondary road. Suddenly a lorry came round the corner, and although we scrambled to the side, we were in full view. Fortunately they were all Italian workmen in the back. It was then that we realised that this was the national road through the mountains, over the La Futa pass linking Bologna and Florence.

The next days we were on Mount Falterone, which is really a group of mountains spread over a 15 by seven mile radius. The following weeks were nearly all spent traversing these mountain ranges, Monte Fumaiola, Monte Nerone and Monte Catria, not far from Gubbio, where Francis of Assisi tamed the wolf that was terrorising the village.

The earlier part of our journey I was able to write about later whilst hiding near the fighting line, but my notes finished at Falterone. So for this next part of the journey I have to rely on my memory 50 years on. It is mainly of mountains, great beauty, lonely farm houses, and occasionally having to cross valleys. The mountains here were barer than in the north, and so there weren't many villages, just the occasional farm house. We would come across bands of Italians forming themselves into guerrilla bands, but at this stage there didn't seem to be much action. I think that came later.

GRAN SASSO

As we came nearer the fighting line, the situation changed. We had to stay in the higher mountains, as the valleys and even the higher villages were full of troops. So we were forced to go up into the deep snows of the Gran Sasso

53

d'Italia. This massive range, the highest south of the Alps, was made famous because Mussolini was held in a resort hotel on the south side of it, whence he was later rescued by German parachute troops.

Up in these deep snows we met with two other escaped prisoners of war, and from them we learnt of a message received by radio which directed escaped prisoners to go to a certain spot, giving a compass bearing and mileage to it, where they would find a parachutist who would guide them through the fighting line. We took this seriously, but it meant climbing over the shoulder of this 8,700-foot range to get to the other side.

This direction took us through a completely deserted valley, and having walked for a day and a half through it, we found at the end we had to climb a cliff to get to the other side. Eventually we did make this climb, and so reached the south-west slope of the Gran Sasso, but in complete mist. In the distance we heard the sound of sheep and a dog and out of the mist came a hooded figure – hooded with a sack to keep the damp mist from his head. He approached us looking very strange and then said in a broad accent, 'Are you boys English or American?' We were both surprised and delighted. This man on the lonely mountainside had been in America like so many others, had saved some money, and bought himself a mountain farm. He was very helpful but warned us that the valley we were going down into was full of German troops and would be very dangerous.

We went on, however, now not walking openly but going through fields and hiding behind bushes. Once we heard a voice call *'Alt'*, but to our relief it was a German sentry stopping a truck in a nearby lane.

As we were wandering through this field we suddenly saw a man watching us and realising we couldn't hide from him, we went up to him. He told us of the danger we were in and then very generously offered to hide us until our troops came. At that point they were about 40 miles to the south. He explained that he was a miner who had worked abroad and that he would make us a grotto in the side of the terraced hill above his house. This was Vittorio Massara, who was to become our friend and guardian for the next three months, whilst we waited for the advance.

Opposite: Plate 1 – Fagnano Alto. The author lived in a cave on a terraced hillside three-quarters of a mile from Fagnano Alto for almost three months without being betrayed. He painted this when he returned after the war.

54

Chapter 5   FRASCARA

THE GROTTO which Vittorio made for us had an entrance four or five feet deep so you had to go on hands and knees to get into it. This led to an area under a rock which was six feet by six, and in which you could just stand up. He made it with great care, with props to hold up the entrance and several lashings of branches which skilfully concealed the way in. He made a rough frame on which he put a mattress and fixed a chimney and fireplace and even a shelf on the wall for our candles and odds and ends. He put a canvas over the top of the roof so that water would-n't drop on to us, a place for a washbowl, a place for a bag of apples and nuts and a couple of water bottles, and even a nail to hang coats on. As he was making it he would stand back and consider how best to arrange it. He looked upon it as a work of art, and so it was. As there was al-ready quite a large hole under the rock he completed the whole thing very quickly. He took the risk of having us in the house during the two days of construction.

The cave was on a terraced hillside above the tiny ham-let of Frascara which consisted of just 15 families. The grotto was so well hidden on one of many terraces that we often had difficulty in finding it ourselves.

Vittorio and his wife Anna were wonderful to us, bring-ing up food for our breakfast and lunch. In the evening we would go down to their house, which was on the edge of the hillside, for a meal with the family, Vittorio, Anna, and Elisa aged eight. I wrote in my diary: 'After the meal Vittorio escorts us back to the grotto. There is a new moon now but for the last fortnight it has been very dark. He takes my arm and leads me as if I were a child. I hold out a stick and Fred comes scrambling on behind.

'When we get to the grotto he lights a candle and if it's cold he lights a fire too. Nothing is too much trouble, and the food is the best he can get. If there is no meat in the evening he is full of apologies. We are indeed fortunate. He is also very careful in not letting it be known outside the village that we are here.'

Opposite: Plate 2 – *Langdale Pikes*

The Grotto painted by
the author 20 years later

During the first days there I went out on my own to search for the signal box where we had been told there would be a parachutist to help us through the fighting line, but without any success. I don't know to this day whether it was a hoax or a genuine message.

After two months the snow fell thick over our hillside and my companion Fred, the tall guardsman from Northumberland, got lumbago, so Vittorio and Anna said that we must come down to the house and live in the back room. This was built against the hillside so that it was possible to escape over its roof and straight into the hills. There was real danger, however, as the nearest German patrol was only a mile away. The danger was almost greater for Vittorio, as the minimum punishment for any family caught harbouring escaped prisoners was to burn their house down and send the menfolk away to a forced labour camp. Our only protection was the friendship of

56

the 15 families of the village and the fact that there was no road to the village. Any vehicle that stopped on the road half a mile away was an immediate signal for us to get up into the woods.

On December 23rd I wrote in my journal: 'Last night I felt rather depressed after one of my host's friends had been in and expressed the opinion that the country between us and our troops was too difficult for an advance during the winter, and that unless there was another landing it would probably be May before our troops arrived. The news rather bore this out as there has been practically no movement for ten days, and all the fighting has been on the coast. The thought of living like this for nearly six months does not fill me with enthusiasm. I feel like making an immediate attempt to cross the line, although it is probably at best a five-to-one chance against getting through. However, as it is useless to make an attempt when the moon is down, we would have to wait until the beginning of next month for the new moon. It's Christmas Eve. I am thinking of all the food we would eat at home and the presents. But perhaps it isn't such a bad thing to celebrate Christmas in a grotto without all these things.

'At this moment my daily prayer of this verse was answered:

> I ask no dream, no prophet ecstasies
> No sudden rending of the veil of clay
> No angel visitant, no opening skies
> But take the dimness of my soul away!

'The clouds are low and grey, unusual for this country, and the steep slope across the river is dark and foreboding, with the black desolate mountains behind, half shrouded in mist, like some Miltonic picture of the universe. The light is fading, and all the villages scattered about the valley seem quiet, not desolate, but as if everyone is at home sitting beside the fire. I am thinking again of Siegfried Sassoon's poem:

> Everyone's voice was suddenly lifted
> And beauty came like the setting sun
> and my heart was moved with tears, and gloom
>   vanished away
> O but everyone was a bird, and the song was
>   wordless
> And the singing will never be done.

'Out of a picture, dull and darkening and rather

57

lonesome, comes that unexplainable joy of heart and spirit:

> I only know there came to me
> A fragrance such as never clings
> To aught save happy living things;
> A sound as of some joyous elf
> Singing sweet songs to please himself.'
>
> (*Renascence* – Edna S Vincent Millay)

Poetry strangely played a big part during the trek. I had pushed into my pack a small paperback anthology called *The Week-End Book* and would read my favourites from it day by day. As paper for toilet purposes was virtually non existent, I had to jettison pages as I went along – but not before endeavouring to commit my favourites to memory. By the end of the journey the book had been used up, but I had been enriched by having learnt the poems I loved best.

'I am writing this in the Massara living room where Vittorio and Fred are teaching each other card games. Anna and Elisa have gone to Mass. The room is about ten feet square, and the walls are painted black and brick coloured, but the plaster is flaked, and the curved top, rather like a ship's cabin, is so black with smoke that the general impression is not of any particular colouring but just of a general dismalness. The flooring is red flag, the furniture a wooden table and five cord bottomed chairs. Around the walls hang two frying pans, two or three enamel bowls, two Italian Army mess tins, an iron and a bit of grating for the fire.

'The fire itself is on a small, very slightly raised, semi-circle of brick in front of a slight indentation from which proceeds the smallest of chimneys. Hanging from the roof is a long bar of iron with links and hooks for holding the big copper pot they use for making the soup. The fire is nearly always low, as there is not much wood round here, so they mainly use it for cooking and then most of the smoke pours into the room. On a small stone shelf rests a polished brass water container. It is a beautiful shape and reflects the rather dim electric light brightly. When Elisa carries it on her head (it is heavy, too) the sight is really delightful. There is no water or bathroom in the house, so every drop has to be carried and the hen house in the basement serves as a lavatory.'

'25th December 1943: Christmas Day. We went to bed at 2.30 this morning after a pleasant and quiet evening, talking and writing. Today we came down from the grotto

58

at 12 noon, and at 1.00 we had a colossal meal. It started with *pastasciuta*, a great plateful, followed by lamb boiled in tomato juice with bread, then kidney, etc., and afterwards roasted lamb and lettuce. The lamb was one of his own, only one and a half months old, and it was beautifully tender. After the meal we had a fifth of a small bar of chocolate, which tasted very good, and then a cup of tea without either sugar or milk.'

'28th December: We have just had a very pleasant interlude – a visit from two American girls – one married to an Italian who is in America, and the other single. They were caught here when America came into the war. They live in Fagnano Alto which is higher up the hillside than our grotto. As their house is the closest to us it is rather comforting to know that they had not noticed us. They said they had seen smoke but hadn't thought much about it.

'They didn't know anything about us being here, but had just called to see Vittorio and Anna. One of them happened to say, "Where are the English now?" meaning the Allied troops. Vittorio, thinking they meant us, put his finger to his lips and then proceeded to produce us from the next room, to which we always escape when there are visitors from another village. They themselves being American citizens are often suspected of being spies.

'We were delighted to meet them and to have a conversation in English.'

'4th February 1944: Yesterday I got up early, washed and shaved off the beard which I had grown (razor blades are hard to come by). I dressed myself in Vittorio's best suit, took off my eye shield and started off to go to the fair in Fontecchio. It was strange to see this village, in which I have been living for two months, for the first time. Actually it is the best built village I've been in. All quite nice houses, the reason being that all except the Massara family and one other have been in America.

'I walked along the path through the fields, greeted the people I passed and was greeted in return without suspicion or undue interest. I remembered John Buchan's book *The Thirty-Nine Steps* in which he says the best disguise is to think and believe yourself the person you are pretending to be. So I thought myself into being a young Italian going to the fair. All the same, as I approached the village and saw groups of people standing about, I wasn't entirely free from nervousness.

'Butch, my host's dog, had followed me, and as I walked down the slope to the road where the people were standing, the dog couldn't quite understand it. He could smell the clothes of his master, but the other scents were different. Elisa Massara, who was staying with her aunt at Fontecchio, passed by and seeing Butch looked round for her father. She glanced at me but failed to recognise me and walked on. I strolled along with my hands in my pockets amongst the groups of people and, leaving the road, walked down into the village. I stopped to read the German news bulletin posted on the wall and was very interested to read a story about British atrocities and the trouble in southern Italy.

'Fontecchio is a German headquarters so there were plenty of German soldiers walking about. Making a tour of the village I found the headquarters, saw where their transport was hidden, their workshops and the places where most of the soldiers were billeted.

'The Germans ignored me in the same way that they ignore the Italians. It is quite a big village situated on the provincial road and built in a ravine sloping downwards the railway and the river. The houses are for the most part old and are built in terraces of as many as five or six storeys. The streets are cobble and mud, and also the usual irregular shape, and the houses are placed haphazardly without plan.

'If you have seen a Cornish fishing village, particularly those towards Lands End, you will have some idea as to what it looks like. Only here there were a lot of very poor and semi-derelict houses, and the little alleyways leading to them were more reminiscent of slums than of a pleasant fishing village. As I walked up the slope past the fountain one of the young girls washing clothes there called up to me. I didn't understand what she said, but seeing the others laugh and the manner in which she said it, I took it to be a joke and smiled back. It was rather fun being treated as an ordinary civilian again, instead of being stared at as a curiosity.

'This year the fair was practically non-existent, two stalls with a few clothes to sell and about half a dozen pigs for sale. That was all. I mingled with the people examining these things and when passing one of the girls from our village smiled at her. She smiled back but with that sort of smile as if to say, I've seen you before, but I don't know just who you are. Seeing Vittorio I went and greeted him, and we stood talking together for a few minutes. As soon as he was joined by others I left him, for if I had to speak more than a few words they would soon be suspicious.

60

'Later he took me into his sister's house, and soon we were joined by Elisa and Anna. Anna told me that the girl of the village I had smiled at had said to her that she had seen a young man at the fair who was rather like the English fellow who lived at their house. We drank some imitation coffee and then all together went up to another part of the village where they were selling earthenware cooking pots. I went into the place and examined the stuff and then with the rest of the menfolk waited outside. It was rather like shopping with my mother or sister in England.

'Wait. Wait. Wait. There were two men standing talking a few yards away, and I thought I heard one of them whisper, "I think that *giovanotto* (young man) there is an American." They stared a little curiously, but I am not sure that I heard them correctly. Later I met the American girl from Fagnano Alto again. She was surprised to see me and rather nervous, telling me to be careful as it was easy to see that with my fair skin and blue eyes I wasn't an Italian. We had lunch at Anna's sister's house and in the late afternoon left Fontecchio and walked home together along the main road and then across the fields to Frascara. To some of the villagers it seems a very foolish thing to do and perhaps they are right, but the information I gathered may be very useful in the next few weeks. A man who goes too carefully never does anything worthwhile.

'Down the valley towards the front line I can get glimpses of snow-covered tops. It is very tantalising, and I wonder what it would have been like if we'd gone on. Apart from the distant rumbling of bombs and very occasionally gunfire, and the odd flight of planes heard overhead, one would never know that there was a war on and that the front line was only 40 miles away.

*   *   *   *   *

'Later. Four of our planes flew very low yesterday and dropped bombs quite near. I think they must have hit an ammunition lorry or train because there were continual explosions afterwards.

*   *   *   *   *

'The last three days have been very strenuous. We went up to the hills behind the village, nearly two hours walk in the snow and cut out patches in the snow in order to signal to our aircraft. This took a lot of digging, but they showed up well. Three Spitfires passed overhead at about 500 feet but gave no sign of having seen them.

'We hoped they might send us boots, food and ammunition. The risk was very small as there are no German or Italian planes in the sky at all.

* * * * *

'Having heard of an RAF squadron leader who was helping escaped POW's, Vittorio and I walked four hours through the snow to meet him. Within sight of the village we stopped and demanded that the squadron leader must come out to see us, as we were afraid that there might be some plot and that he might be bogus. After rather a long time we at last caught sight of men coming from the village, and seeing only two we went to meet them. It was good to meet another Englishman after more than two months of seeing only Italians. His story was very interesting. He was a squadron leader in the RAF, and he had been dropped at the Brenner at the Armistice, one of many charged with managing the various schemes in operation to help prisoners and to liberate Italy. Nearly all these schemes fell through, and he was in a very similar position to us. So he took a train from there to Milan, dyed his hair black and greased his skin. (His hair is fair, and he has a very fair skin.) Then he took the train south as far as he could, which was Ancona. From there he made his way to this area and since then has been working around, helping prisoners and passing information over his radio.

'His main work has been getting medicine, but he has also bought a lot of shoes from the Germans for our people. He speaks good Italian and German. There are over 100 prisoners living in the villages in his area, more to the south of here, and so he keeps quite busy visiting them and looking after them. We had hoped to get some arms through him, but he has tried signalling and though the signals are acknowledged nothing has been sent. Apparently a lot of stuff dropped has fallen into the wrong hands and so they are not dropping any more.

'He gave me a detailed picture of the fighting at the moment and what he thought would happen in the near future. Before the landing north of Rome, when our troops were stationary, there was a lot of trouble with spies. He told me about two officers from my camp who were living in a hut in the mountains. This squadron leader was living in a hut nearby.

'Two Germans dressed in civilian clothes had gone to the village below, which was supplying them with food, and asked a villager, "Where are our companions? We are escaped English prisoners." The man replied that they were living in a hut in the mountains.

'The two Germans then produced weapons, revealed their identity to the man and said, "You will accompany us to their place of hiding." The man, very frightened, took them up to the hut and knocked on the door. It was opened by a captain who was greeted by several rounds of lead. He died immediately, and the wounded lieutenant was taken prisoner. The next day, by sheer coincidence (a mistake on the part of a British pilot), the house of the man who had given them away was machine gunned, and one of the family was wounded.'

Chapter 6   OVER THE MAIELLA

ONE DAY after almost three months in Frascara we heard, 'There's an American coming to see you.' We were immediately anxious. So many were caught by that phrase. Expecting to welcome another escaped prisoner, they were met by a German dressed in civilian clothes who, by pretending to be a British or American, had been led to them and so had taken them prisoner again.

So we prepared for him and placed ourselves behind doors armed with heavy sticks, to take a good look at him and hear his voice before meeting him. There was no mistaking him as he entered. He was as American as they come, with a lively spirit – a fighter pilot who had 'dropped out of the sky'.

Roane and I became friends and we decided to get over the line together. Fred's boots had long since given out and all our efforts to signal the RAF to drop boots for us had failed, so sadly he had to stay behind. Later I heard from him that after many narrow escapes he had been freed as the Allies advanced. Although from completely different backgrounds we had become good companions. We wrote once or twice but my last letter was returned 'not known at this address'. I was very sorry to lose touch with him as we had been through all these adventures together.

The only place Roane and I thought worth trying was the Maiella, a mountain range lying under six feet of snow that year and with one ski patrol (we understood) for the whole 15 miles of mountain, and on the other side – the Allies.

Diary, 14th March: 'The parting from Frascara and from Vittorio, Anna, and Eliza was rather like leaving home. Ever since I have talked about going, they have besieged me with all the reasons for staying. Everyone in the village, where we have felt so much at home, has been very kind. The school teacher who lived next door went round every family, and all of them subscribed to give us a present of money. We'd never had any money before, apart from two English pounds that I'd kept, and in fact we had never had occasion to need money or to spend it, as all our needs had been provided for by the gifts of the mountain farmers. As we left they also showered us with food for the journey.'

16th March: 'Setting off again was like putting the clock back three months and getting used to life "on the road" once more.

'A man called Paolo from a nearby village, who knew the area near the Maiella, agreed to guide us.

'The next days were the most uncomfortable and the most dangerous we'd ever had, as we had to go right through the middle of the German supply lines and also cross a major river. It meant walking at night and then during the day finding any kind of shelter we could. It was generally too cold to sleep, and we were glad to move on again and get warm by moving as rapidly as we could along the rough mountainsides.

'At one point we couldn't find any water to drink and our thirst was terrific until finally we came across snow and began to eat it. We felt better but it doesn't really quench the thirst. For most of the journey we were scrambling along the hillsides as it was much too dangerous to be on any track in the valley. Eventually we got near to the village in the foothills of the Maiella where Paolo had friends. From here we could see the great white expanse of the mountain range.

'Paolo went off to see if he could find a guide to take us over the top, whilst we sheltered in a cold shack in the corner of a field. We waited there three days, and each evening he would come back and tell us he hadn't been successful. We suspected that he was negotiating terms for taking us over as he was keen to benefit himself from it. Our food was getting low. We had only about three days' supply left, and we felt also that we might well be discovered by some of the German troops. We even wondered whether we would be forced to return to Frascara.

'Eventually Paolo came running to the hut and said we would have to hurry to catch a party which was just about to set off. So we scrambled along the fields and reached the rendezvous, a group of two or three barns and cattle sheds, only to find that the party had already gone. However, as we were wondering what to do, a young Italian fellow of about 30 approached and, after making sure who we were, told us that he and his companions were just about to set off to cross the mountain.'

Our Italian friends were very light hearted, but rather

unprepared for a climb of that kind and far too noisy. They were mostly middle class – two officers, a solicitor, and an engineer. Two were Sicilians, two were from Rome, and the rest from this area, nine in all. Two were wearing shoes and thin socks, and several were carrying suitcases. It was more like a party going on a picnic than an attempt to cross a front line. We asked them where the guide was and rather gathered that he was somewhere ahead.

We had been travelling for about an hour when we found that there was in fact no guide and that all they knew of the mountains had been learned from a very inadequate map. Roane and I did not think of turning back but decided that we would keep our eyes wide open and go off on our own if we did not like the way things were shaping.

We climbed up along a steep valley following a narrow footpath. It was a clear moonless night, and we could just make out where the path ran along an upward curving ledge on the steep side. I walked behind Roane so that his white socks would give me some help where to put my feet. With only one eye functioning I found this rather difficult to judge. After less than an hour's walking we had our first rest, and after about another half hour we reached the snow. That meant another rest while the Italians debated whether we should go on or not. At every stop there was always someone who wanted to make a fire.

It was a fascinating climb, especially as we got higher amongst the snow and could see the steep white glistening slopes shining out as a contrast to the dark, starlit sky. Presently we left the path and climbed up a slope to cross a narrow snow-covered mountain road. We could see the lights of the last civilian-occupied village. Once across the road we were assured that all danger from the Germans was past. The next hour's climb was steep, but the frozen snow covered by an inch of soft snow was easy climbing.

We reached the top of this slope, and there stretching above us, like a sheet on a clothes line, we could see the long ridge of mountains. We were able to pick out the very slight dip through which it was proposed that we should pass. It had the rather ominous name of Grotto del Uomo Morto (Dead Man's Gully). Between us and the white ridge we could see trees, and the whole thing looked close and easy. But we knew this was an illusion; mountains over 8,000 feet under deep snow were not going to be child's play. Once we reached the woods we started the

67

hard work. The snow here was not frozen to the same extent, and at every step we sank at least two feet, and many times above the knees. This was hard work particularly for the leading man. Roane and I did well over our share of this as well as carrying a case for the engineer. Our kit was light, as we carried nothing but our food reserve.

We had to stop frequently as one of the Italians with low shoes was feeling really ill, chiefly due to his feet being frozen. My feet were fairly comfortable in spite of the fact that the sole of my right boot was half off and the stitching of the uppers adrift. I wrapped a spare sock round the boot. It froze over the gap, and this prevented the snow from entering into my boot.

On and on we went, plodding through the trees towards that all too white ridge. The going was nearly all bad and, except for very occasional treeless patches where we sunk only about a foot, it was all deep snow. The depth of snow must have been six feet, but the lower snow was frozen, leaving about two feet of soft snow on the top.

At three o'clock in the morning we reached the last belt of trees, and we reckoned that another hour's climbing would bring us to the final climb. At this stage the fire-makers won the round, and in spite of our protests they made a fire on the snow. It took some time to get it going, but once on its way it made a really big fire. We sat huddled around it, and as it burnt we watched it drop lower and lower into the snow. It kept my front warm, but the thin liningless mackintosh I was wearing was little use against the icy wind that swirled round the back. Eventually the fire sank so low into the snow that there was not enough air for it to burn, and so they started to build another fire. That meant another twenty minutes of freezing cold until the fire got going again. Much as we disliked the Italians' methods, I could not help admiring them.

They laughed and talked when there should have been absolute quietness; they argued at every stage as to the best way to go; they made a fire in the middle of the night. All wrong, but one could not help being grateful for the spirit of men who set out to cross an 8,000-foot snow covered ridge, which was also a battle line, in low, unnailed shoes, without any hardening up process and no previous experience of the mountains.

It was half past five before we left the fire, and the sky was growing lighter every minute. This was our final assault and from our position underneath the slope I began to think it would take more than the three hours we had estimated. Paolo was leading the way. Roane and I remained at the back, as we were far from sharing the Italians' confidence that the mountain was our only barrier to freedom, and we thought this was the safest place.

We had only gone a few minutes when Roane said that he smelt smoke. Further up he said that he could see ski marks in the snow above the belt of trees. At this stage Paolo was tired and he called out for Roane to go up and lead. As it turned out, this was very fortunate. After about another quarter of an hour, Roane motioned for everyone to stop and be quiet. He was still well ahead of us, and he started to come back. In spite of his warning the Italians started calling and shouting to each other, and it took rather angry words on my part to stop them.

Roane made his way back, a slow process in the deep snow, and spoke to the group, telling them about the smoke which could now be smelt by everyone. Also the ski marks were more apparent and finally we could hear voices. The party decided to go on, but we said we would follow at an interval and handed the engineer his case, which we had carried for him all the time. Paolo hardly knew what to do, but eventually decided to go on with the others. I think he was influenced by the thought that to be caught with two ex-POWs was too risky. We started to dig holes in the snow to hide in, then decided it would be safer to scramble over to the left, going towards the dip on the mountain ridge. The original idea had been to go straight up through the trees, and when we reached the harder snow to make along to the left.

We lost sight of the party when we got amongst the trees because of a dip in the ground. A few minutes later Roane pointed them out to me again. We stopped to watch them and to get our breath, and decided there must be Germans with them as we thought there were more than ten.

The party was divided into three groups, but as we could not see all the group at once, we were not quite sure of it. Pepi, one of the Italians we had made friends with, was in the nearest group about 150 yards away and Roane in a fit of madness called out to him. I quickly hushed him, as by now it was obvious something was up. Fortunately, Pepi did not hear, nor apparently did anyone else.

A moment or two later we saw that one of the three parties had stopped at a snow dugout, and we could now pick out the white-clothed German ski troops. We were in snow and the trees between us were few. I am not sure of the distance. It just seemed too close. We could not have been more than 300 yards away from the snow shelter. We got down in the snow and hoped that the Germans would not look our way. Fortunately, they were very busy talking to their prisoners.

When they started to move they went at right angles to us, and we then made our escape and floundered through the snow away from them as fast as we could go. Most of the way we simply rolled over and over in the snow so that very little of us showed. We had only gone a short distance when we reached a pulley arrangement going down the mountain and alongside which were much-used tracks, obviously made by skis. We lay down in these for a moment as this was the first time we had been out of the sight of the Germans. I suggested that we should move on in case anyone should come along these tracks and we pushed rather breathlessly on.

Suddenly Roane gripped my arm and instinctively I fell flat into the snow. I did not dare move and so could not see what was happening, but Roane whispered in my ear that four Germans and a number of Italians were passing down the track. We were nearer to them than before, and it was a miracle that they did not see us. Again I felt that I had been saved by Roane's keen senses. Never did I feel more grateful to anyone. We remained there until they were well down the track and then dashed off as fast as we could in case others were following them.

We thought at first that it might be our late companions they were taking down, but it seemed rather too soon, even considering how much faster one can move in tracks compared with rolling and scrambling through untouched snow. On and on we went until we lay in a place where there was a certain amount of cover from the trees.

We still thought it might be possible to get over the line, as the Germans were a long way to the right of the dip. As we lay there our hopes were shattered. Going up a hardly visible track, sloping from the shelter to the dip in the ridge, were four figures – Germans. We then thought we could go further along the ridge, well away from the Germans, and then climb the highest part of the ridge.

As we scrambled on the going became worse as the snow was softer, and also there were only two of us to take a turn in leading. Many times we floundered up to our waists in the snow and had to tug each other out. Eventually we came to a treeless part, but this was even worse as it was frozen. Once I slipped and started sliding down.

70

This was not a long or steep slope but shortly afterwards, when we reached a longer steep slope to cross, we really felt nervous. It was just about this time that Roane spotted a party of about 50 or 60 people going up the ski track. A moment later we saw another party of about the same size down in the valley below moving like ants in the direction in which we guessed the ski track would end.

Although both of us wanted to tackle this last part of the Maiella, knowing that we were within a few miles of the Allies, we were now aware also that the slopes were icy and that there were more Germans on the mountain than we had realised.

We rested for a moment on this icy slope whilst we considered what to do. I quietly prayed for direction. The thought came like a flash, 'Go back. Go back.' Roane quickly agreed, and we started back. It was 18 hours' walk in deep snow before we reached the foot of the mountain again. We spent the night in a hayloft, dead to the world with tiredness.

As we woke in the morning we discovered that a party waiting to go over the Maiella had shared the loft with us. We met one of this party, an Italian would-be escapee over the mountains, and he told us there was a professor in Sulmona who organised parties. I followed him into Sulmona to find the *professore*.

Right past the German headquarters, down some side streets to a courtyard and up some steps we went, to the third floor, with my guide always 50 yards ahead, it being too risky for him to be with me. After a hurried consultation at the door he left, and I approached the *professore* not knowing whether this was a trap, and he not knowing whether to trust me. Soon we both felt confident, and very shortly I was hurrying back to the base of the mountains to find Roane, who had spent the day in a cave, and to bring him to Sulmona to join a party leaving for the Maiella that night.

It was interesting that walking into Sulmona I had walked unhurriedly like a peasant, and no one had commented. This time hurrying and taking long strides, several people working in the fields had called out '*Inglese, Americano*' even though my clothes were exactly the same. I darkened Roane's hair with mud, taught him to walk as a peasant, and into Sulmona we went.

As we passed the German headquarters, two Italian boys greeted him and, guessing who he was, walked with him, which was a good shield for him. Soon we were off,

71

together with twelve Italians, three South Africans, and a Scots boy, and led at this point by three guides.

THE FINAL CLIMB

Our route was slightly different to the one we had taken two nights before, being probably safer but not as direct. We had a couple of hours in difficult snow. Then we had to scramble down a steep bank and cross a stream. This was taxing as it was a moonless night. I missed most of the stepping stones, but very little water got into my boots.

Then we climbed up and crossed the snow–covered mountain road just at first light. We had been told we would spend the day in a hut and were delighted to find that it was a well-built refuge hut in a gully about a mile above the road. It was hidden from the last inhabited village, and the guides assured us there were very few Germans around that area.

Roane and I were still very tired after our previous attempt; we had also walked for another 12 hours since leaving Sulmona. We tried to get some sleep, realising that that evening we had to tackle the top of the mountain. We also ate up some of our reserves of food, hoping it would give us more energy for the climb.

That morning two of the guides had left us, promising to return towards five o'clock, but by eight o'clock there was still no sign of them. The only people we could see were a shepherd and two parties of two, each of whom we watched very anxiously for half an hour. They were about two or three miles away. As night came on and the guides failed to come back we became rather despondent. Marco, the guide left with us, had never been over this particular way before and he could not take us on his own.

At half past eight an energetic little man who introduced himself as Mario arrived. He was apparently the big noise of the party and had made many trips. He seemed very annoyed that we were so few, and especially that so few of us were escaped prisoners, as it seemed that he received 5,000 lire (about £12) for each prisoner he took over to the Allies. There seemed to be some doubt as to whether he would take the Italians, but after some talk, and the exchange of considerable sums of money, he agreed.

Even then, the project seemed very doubtful, as Mario was worried about the weather. He claimed to have taken over parties of 200, although this was the first time he had

72

taken a party over this way. He said that he knew the mountains well.

Next, one of the two guides who had gone to the village returned, and explained that they had been stopped by the Germans. He had been able to bluff his way out, but his colleague had been taken off to a concentration camp.

At nine o'clock we set off. Everything inspired confidence. The guides, three in all, were amazingly efficient, one in front, one in the middle, and the last at the rear. And this time there was no deep snow to plough through. They knew where the snow was hard and, except for bad patches for a few hundred yards, we walked in less than a foot of soft snow. It had been cloudy all day, and although the clouds looked thinner now there was a nasty cold wind.

The guides said it would take five hours from here to make the top and between six and seven hours to the other side where our troops were. We were on a moderately steep slope at this part, but travelling was slow as the big South African's legs were giving him trouble. Eventually Roane and the tall guide Paolo had to help him along. This went on for over half an hour and our pace became dreadfully slow.

Finally the South African had to stop and after a conference we decided that he would have to go back. He was a game fellow and except for his legs felt fit enough, but it was plain that undernourishment was doing its work and that he would never make it. His friend offered to go back with him, but he would not hear of it. I felt very guilty leaving him there half way up the mountainside, but there seemed no alternative. I gave him all the money I had, two English pounds and some lire, and it was arranged that he should go back to the last village and wait there until the guides returned, getting all the food he could and building up his strength for the next party. We never heard what happened to him.

About ten minutes after we left him the stiff climb began. I have always been fond of climbing and heights have never worried me in the slightest, but this was new and different. Mario went first, digging into the frozen snow with his boots, trudging about 15 paces slanting up to the left and then to the right. He had chosen a place sheltered from the wind so that the icy snow was softer, but even so the footholds were not very deep. This is the part of the Maiella which I described earlier as looking like a sheet on a clothes line, and the angle of the mountain at

73

close quarters was just as frightening as it had looked at a greater distance.

When we paused and looked up what we saw were figures above moving on a never-ending white surface up into the sky. I climbed a large part of the way with my two feet on the ground but with one hand against the icy slope. I had lent Roane one of my gloves and so, as we changed direction, I leaned first on one hand and then on the other, changing my woollen glove at the same time. Ten minutes of this might have been fun but two hours was a nerve-racking nightmare. One slip and you would slide hundreds of feet down, and it seemed so easy to slip. At one period Paolo saw me stumbling up very slowly in this way, and told me to hang on to his pack and he would lead me up. He had good nails in his boots and an ice stick, and although it did not feel too safe it helped to increase my confidence. I then realised why I had been led not to tackle the top slope on our own.

Eventually the slope became less steep and the snow softer; it was little more than 45°, and we were able to go straight up it. There was a lot of moaning and lagging behind at this stage; some of the Italians were getting very tired, and I think their nerves were as bad as ours.

It was also becoming increasingly difficult to see, as we were in cloud at this height. Up and up we went, thinking at every point that we must be at the top, but all that happened was that the slope became less steep. At about one o'clock we were told that we were at the top, and it was a matter of going up and down now across the undulating tops. The wind here was icy, the mist was thick, and it had been snowing spasmodically for the last hour. Both Roane and I at this point felt very fit, and we took up positions near the leading guide, determined that at any rate *we* would stick to him and not get left with any detached parties. The soft snow here was over a foot thick and the going bad.

Everything began to freeze in that wind. I tied my scarf round my hat and neck to keep my hat on, and to keep my ears from freezing. My hair, which fell over my forehead, collected the snow and froze into a fringe of icicles. My eyebrows froze, my eyes watered and the wind froze my eyelashes. My boots had been frozen for some time but now my trousers, mack and scarf also froze.

I cannot say how long we had been going before I realised that two of our party were far from well, but it must have been at about half past one. At any rate we had been

74

wandering over the tops for something like half an hour in what had now become a blizzard, stopping every few yards to let the others catch up. The guide's course seemed to have become a bit irregular. During the climb I had remarked to Roane that Mario must be brilliant to find his way in the dark and in mist over a snow capped top. Now I suspected he had lost his way, but it was some time before he would admit it.

Just after this the party stopped again, and Roane and I went back to find that one of the South Africans had collapsed. We set about rubbing him, hands, face and neck, and after a short time he began to come round. The only thing possible was to keep walking, for if we stopped for more than a few minutes it was very doubtful if we would survive. Paolo took on the job of helping him along, and I helped his friend, the other South African, who was in a similar state. We had only stumbled a few yards through the snow before he collapsed.

We gathered a few people round and rubbed him back to life. He could not see as his eyes were frozen tight. His frozen hands were like lumps of raw meat. I put a glove on one of his hands and put the other through my mack to try and keep them from frost bite. My own hands were kept alive by putting one in my pocket and the other under his arm as I half carried him along.

The Scotsman, who was also nearly exhausted, came along and took the other side of him, and so we stumbled on. At every step we rubbed life back into the two poor chaps, and then we half carried them on. It kept us warm too, and our supply of energy seemed unlimited. I remember reviewing the situation in my mind and thinking I could keep walking till morning, and if I kept moving I shouldn't die. I had given up hope of the two South Africans pulling through unless we could find shelter from the wind.

At about half past three they both collapsed completely. We gathered a few of the party around one of the South Africans, to keep the wind off him, and started the rubbing again. I put my cheek against his frozen cheek and with my body rubbed against his and got the Italians to do the same. He came round and could hardly talk, but his constant question was for his friend. I kept replying, with very false confidence, that his friend was all right, and that he himself would pull through. In actual fact I believed at the time that his friend was dying. He had fallen into the snow like a log, and the other Italians were round him

75

sheltering him with their coats while Roane and the tall guide attempted to bring him round.

It was fortunate that here there seemed to be a little shelter from the wind, and I suppose we must have stopped there for half an hour. The Italians in my party kept moving round to the sheltered side, and it was only when I got really angry with them that they moved to shelter him again. Mario, who knew the mountain well, said that it was clearly hopeless and that we couldn't survive.

Miraculously, the South Africans came round again. We started to drop down a bit, and the wind was rather less fierce, though it continued to snow. The 17 dark figures battling in the snow the previous evening had now become white phantoms covered with queer icicles and for the most part grouped in threes.

The snow on this side was softer, and the going was very bad, but that may have been a blessing in disguise as the movement generated some heat in our bodies, and I believe it was more the cold than the exhaustion that had played havoc with us. Presently the sky began to lighten, and we started to think that the battle was nearly won.

The only trouble was that we did not know where we were, except that we were over 8,000 feet up on the top of a mountain ridge that stretched many miles. Mario led us blindly on, changing direction every few minutes, and there was a lot of angry talk and arguing. Roane and I had previously thought that it might be necessary to make straight down to the nearest village, friendly or otherwise, and get the two South Africans attended to, but as dawn came their strength seemed to return, and we thought once more of the possibility of reaching our line.

After a considerable amount of scrambling around we called a halt and Roane produced the little escape compass he had, and the map – a difficult process with half frozen hands and with the wind and snow still blinding us. Mario had a slight idea of map reading, and he was able to say which area was in British hands. We took a general bearing from the area in which we believed we were, to the first British-occupied village, and then pointed out the direction to him. It took some time before he was able to keep that direction.

It should have been easy, as the wind was blowing constantly and fiercely from the same quarter, but he was accustomed to seeing his way, and the thick mist and snow baffled him. Our bearing took us along the side of the

76

mountain but descended steadily until the mist began to get thinner.

I shall never forget seeing a snow-covered rocky ridge appearing through the mist in front of us. It was the first time we had seen any shape since the previous night, and we rather expected that Mario would be able to tell us where we were. However, it was too much to hope that he knew every rock, and so we went on steadily bearing downwards. Eventually we began to see the form of hills around us, and Mario once more knew where we were.

We were still half carrying the two South Africans, but daylight and the hope of freedom had given them a new lease of life, and in the hours that followed they were bolstered up and kept going by this hope.

Eventually we dropped down into a steep sided valley, and by this time the weather was clear. We went cautiously for fear of enemy patrols and when within sight of a road sent one of the Italians forward to reconnoitre. He waved us on, and we reached the road and looked down on to a ruined village.

Every building, including the church, was a wreck, and it was deserted. The bridge over the river had been blown up, and the road itself destroyed at every possible point. We didn't know in which direction we would find our troops and in which the Germans. We sent one man ahead who said he could identify the tyre marks. He came back and said the Allies were to the left. We clambered off the road. We had no alternative, as the tunnel through which it ran had been destroyed.

After some scrambling we reached the road on the left side. There were tyre marks here, and Roane swore that they were made by American tyres. The destroyed village lay down the hillside to our right, and we watched it carefully as we went towards Palumbaro. All we saw were two people in Italian uniform who might have been on either side, and one whom we thought might be an Indian.

When in sight of Palumbaro we stopped again, and one of the Italians went forward and asked a little girl who was there, British or Germans, she replied British, or at least Indians, and on we went. We were right in the village before we were stopped by an Italian with a rifle who wanted to know who we were. He took us along to the Indian lieutenant who was in the village, and almost in a stupor we introduced ourselves and asked for a cup of tea.

Moments like that, a moment I had dreamed of for two years, are always something of an anti-climax. It was

77

impossible for me to realise that I was free. In fact it took me several days before I was fully aware of it.

I never did know the names of the South Africans or of the Scots boy, so we lost touch with them entirely. When back in Naples I made enquiries whether two South Africans had been admitted to hospital and was assured that they had survived with only minor frostbite.

BACK IN THE ARMY

It was like stepping back two years into the familiar world of the army. Tea was short at the front, but they spared some of their precious rations for us. That first cup of tea, after months without, tasted out of this world.

That night we collapsed into some blankets in a camp on the seashore and slept, and slept, and slept. I woke for just long enough to take some food the next day, and to write a note to my parents, and then went off to sleep again. It was not surprising. We had hardly slept during the four days we had taken to reach the bottom of the Maiella, because we'd had to walk at night and shelter in the daytime in the cold reed huts at the side of the fields. Then during the last four nights we'd had just one night's sleep, although a good one, as we'd made those two attempts to climb the mountain.

The next day Roane was whisked off to an American base, with pneumonia. A few days later I was on my way to Naples, there to land in the middle of a typhoid epidemic and be given every kind of injection ever invented, or so it seemed.

On the first Sunday of my stay in Naples, I woke up early, and as I sat in the quiet of the morning looking out on the Bay of Naples, a simple thought came – go to the Methodist club and the service there. So I went, and chatting with the padre in charge, I told him where I'd come from, and he asked me if I would speak to the soldiers who dropped in for tea in the afternoon. I agreed, and then came the thought – tell them also the part that the guidance of God played in your escape.

When the time came, I yarned to them and told them as much as security would allow, and then suddenly I remembered this thought. So with a bit of a gulp, I said to them, 'Before the war I learned that in any situation, if I wanted and was ready to obey, God could put thoughts into my mind. This was the secret of how I escaped and came those 700 miles.' The men listened attentively, on the edge of their chairs. When I had finished, a soldier came up to me and asked, 'Have you ever been in touch with Moral Re-Armament?' Eagerly I said, 'Yes, I have,' and with a warm shake of the hand he said, 'Well, I have worked with Moral Re-Armament too.'

To me it seemed the fulfilment of the direction I had had to get back to my friends in MRA, and it was eagerly that I asked for all the news of what had been happening. As I mentioned earlier, before the war I had met the Oxford Group, later known as Moral Re-Armament or MRA, who had introduced me to the idea of listening to God which had proved to be so important to me in my escape. For more than two years I had had no news. The Nazis had persecuted the people of MRA because of their uncompromising stand against them and my family, knowing this, had always carefully avoided any mention of it in letters in case it would put me in danger. My friend showed me some new books that had been published, and I believe that it was from him that I first learnt of the remarkable change in the journalist Peter Howard, who had gone to meet people of MRA in order to attack them. For me, however, the meeting meant very much more than just getting news of my friends, important though that was. It made me surer than ever of the way God was leading, that within a few days of getting through the lines I had been led straight to this man.

Shortly after, I left Italy and sailed for England landing at Glasgow docks. Two weeks later I was at last walking through the front door of my home. I must have pictured that moment of arriving a hundred times. It was always the finale of every marvellous escape that I'd dreamt up. Walking through that front door was the climax, and now it had really happened.

PART II
HOME AGAIN

Chapter 7   ENGLAND

IT WAS wonderful to be home again with my mother, father and sister, and all my relations and friends at Fleetwood. This fishing port in Morecambe Bay is where I'd been born and brought up and where my family had lived for four generations.

My great grandfather, who came from Mousehole near Lands End in Cornwall, held a Captain's ticket and had been appointed first mate on the Fleetwood-Belfast service when it started. So he had decided to settle in Fleetwood, then a very small town. He brought his wife and my grandfather aged one, in a small fishing smack, sailing all the way up the west coast with his precious cargo. I suppose it was the most economical way of transporting family and household goods.

The family grew with the town. My grandfather became deputy controller of the port and was active in local politics, becoming the chairman of the Fleetwood Council, whilst the port became the third largest fishing centre in Britain with 120 trawlers going out into the Irish Sea and as far north as Iceland.

With his Cornish Methodist roots he was also prominent in establishing the Wesleyan Methodist Chapel. So my upbringing was strongly Methodist. The chapel was the centre of our lives, not only on Sunday, when we went four times to Sunday School and chapel services; we also went regularly to different activities during the week. I don't remember resenting it, as all our friends did the same, and even after chapel on a Sunday evening we would all gather in our home for sandwiches and to sing hymns around the piano.

Fleetwood was in many ways a place with two separate identities. There was the part where we lived towards the west which was middle class – teachers, bank clerks, office workers, trawler owners, with a smattering of doctors, dentists, lawyers and solicitors. Some of its social life revolved around our Methodist tennis club. Then there was the area centred around the fishing industry, the trawlermen, the dock workers and fish merchants, and all that went with it. The trawlers went out for two to three weeks at a time. The crews would come in for just two or three days between the trips and for many of them it was one great binge. So in the area near the docks there was much drunkenness and loose living. My sister Dorothy, who later became the headmistress of a school near a council estate, had to deal with the effects of all this on the local families.

LAYING THE FOUNDATIONS

Growing up it often felt as if I, too, lived in two different worlds. There was the safe and secure one of a loving family and of home and church and friends, and then there was this rough world which I encountered at the council school where I wasn't really accepted and was bullied and felt like an outsider.

When I went to the Fleetwood Grammar School at the age of 11 this altered a bit, although again with my up-bringing of not swearing or telling dirty stories, I was far from being accepted.

One incident happened on my first day there which was to make life difficult. We had been told firmly that we were not to move from our seats. I was so scared that even though I wanted to go to the lavatory I didn't have the courage to ask, so eventually to my dismay and those around me, I wet my pants. This resulted in a great deal of teasing and my being called 'Sally wet pants' which seemed to go on right through my time at the school.

I remember vividly coming into the last stretch of the quarter mile race and with delight finding that extra surge of pace in order to win it and secure the senior champion-ship. I passed the grandstand, to the cheers of my house, when at the moment of triumph a voice sang out, 'Good old Sally'. I felt so deflated.

I think that it was at this stage of my life that the drive for success started. I was so determined to be popular that I drove myself to excel at sport and would train hard, go-ing out on winter evenings in rain and wind to run round the sea wall in front of our house. In the following years I did succeed in twice becoming sports champion for my age group, and cross country champion, captain of my house, and a member for two seasons of the school rugby 1st XV. Spurred on by this desire to be accepted I also found a girl friend – but with all this I never felt that I was liked.

A great feature of our early years were the summer

holidays. We would let our house, which was on the promenade, for the month of August and so be able to take wonderful holidays in North Wales, Cornwall, or the Isle of Man. It was on these holidays that we met up with the Children's Special Service Mission run by Scripture Union. For me it was a new world. There we met children from public schools and the undergraduates from Oxford and Cambridge who ran these holiday events. They were people of a kind I hadn't met before – charming and cultured. One ill-effect was that I longed to go to a public school, which we couldn't possibly afford, and began to try and lose my Fleetwood accent. But more than that it seemed that for the first time I met people whose Christianity was joyful and contagious. This was particularly true when we went for four summers to Port St Mary in the Isle of Man. The enterprise there, which consisted of short lively services on the beach, swimming parties, games and expeditions, was run by a Dublin solicitor called Matheson, whose joyous Christianity became a pattern for me. His love of God and overflowing care for people has remained in my mind ever since. This gave me the desire to be a Christian, but it wasn't until I met the Oxford Group in 1934 that I understood what it meant.

This meeting happened through one of our Methodist ministers from Blackpool, Cecil Rose, who came occasionally to have lunch with us. He was a rather cool intellectual type who quite suddenly became different. He told us it was because he had read a book called *For Sinners Only* about the Oxford Group. My sister Dorothy and I were intrigued, and accepted an invitation to a weekend gathering in the nearby town of Cleveleys. My sister and I were

85

As a young man   *With his father, mother and sister*

close friends and did many things together. There we met some of Cecil Rose's friends, and through their help I began to look at my life in the light of Christ's standards of absolute honesty, purity, unselfishness and love which they emphasised. I wanted their freedom and sense of purpose. The decisive moment was when I met a young architecture student in Preston, where I had started work in the treasurer's department of the Lancashire County Council. We sat on a park bench overlooking the River Ribble and at his suggestion I wrote down the areas in my life where I didn't come up to these standards.

The most difficult thought that came on this occasion was about my relationship with my parents. Although our home was a happy one, we lived with taboos – the main one being that sex was never even mentioned. It was inconceivable that my parents would talk to me about what were called 'the facts of life' – the phrase would not even have been voiced in our home. I remember, as a boy of, I suppose, six or seven years of age, my mother and I met up with a young woman we knew outside our house, who proudly showed us her new baby. One of the friends with her said, 'Isn't she a lovely baby girl.' I innocently asked, 'Oh, how can you tell whether it's a boy or a girl?' I was then conscious of half-hidden smiles and embarrassment from my mother, but I don't think it occurred to my parents to enlighten me.

Opposite: Plate 3 – Evening Light, Fleetwood

86

We lived in a world where these realities, and also the realities of feelings and emotions, were kept under cover. I still feel a certain reticence myself about some of these things. I know my son suffered at school because I never talked to him fully about sex – presuming that this would have been told him by his teachers.

The other factor in my life was that many of our good Methodist disciplines had become doctrines. We were brought up to believe that drinking a glass of beer was as bad as telling a lie – or that playing a game on Sunday was as bad as a dirty joke, although in fact a dirty joke would never have even been referred to directly. This all contributed to the sense of a barrier, a wall, behind which we could be secure.

It was because of this background, loving but strict, that I found it almost impossible to talk to my parents about my girl friend, my difficulties with sex and also the small deceits I'd practised. Such was the strength of my upbringing that I would never tell a lie, but I would find ways of avoiding telling the whole truth.

So this thought I'd written down on that park bench, to be honest with my parents, was the greatest hurdle. For several days I agonised as to whether I would obey. In fact it was the only time in my life when I walked in my sleep, such was the conflict.

Finally I decided to take this first step. I remember standing outside the living room and praying to be given the strength to be honest. It was much more frightening than climbing through the second-storey window of the prison camp in the dark, not knowing whether I would go crashing to the ground or be shot at by the guards. Equally I didn't know what the reaction of my parents would be. However, the result was almost unbelievable.

My mother was an active church worker, but she had never, to my knowledge, talked about matters of faith. She said to me that day, 'I would like to find the faith you've found,' and I think in subsequent years she did find something of that. My father, who was a man of real faith, responded wholeheartedly. Later he started to tell me things about his own life and his faith which he'd never told anyone – certainly not my mother. He was a help to me as I started then to put right other things in my life.

Although the barrier was breached it was always a difficult decision for me to share with them the deeper and real things in my life. But this was a turning point. I became

Opposite: Plate 4 – Cumbrian river

aware for the first time that there was a power available to give me the courage to do what seemed impossible.

*   *   *   *   *

In the years from 1934 until the war I met just a few associates of the initiator of the Oxford Group, Frank Buchman. I went to one or two weekend house parties. I remember one at Southport – I went without lunches that week so that I could afford it. I also went abroad for the first time, to the Netherlands, and took part with thousands of others in a mass gathering at Utrecht. I sold my grandfather's stamp collection, which he had given me, to pay for the trip.

Mostly I had to find my own way. My Methodist upbringing helped, and good friends like Garth and Corinne Williams were also a great help. My father, whom I got to know more closely, was also supportive, as for instance when he told me that he too as a young man had had to make restitution for something he had pinched.

I was able to win a few people to a Christian commitment, but because I made many mistakes I also put a lot of people off! I decided that whether I was tired or not, I would get up for a quiet time every morning when I would try to listen to God; that was a very important decision.

Then came 1938 and the Munich crisis and finally war in 1939. Our minister at the time was an ardent pacifist and the whole environment of our church seemed to be largely pacifist. When I was called up I was in a dilemma and, not knowing what to do, I first registered as a Conscientious Objector. I prayed about this in my time of quiet and eventually it became clear to me that I should enlist in the services. This decision was made entirely on my own and without any outside pressure either way. Several of my close friends today took a different decision at that time and became Conscientious Objectors, and I respect their decision.

One major thought in my mind was that it was our selfish attitude as a country that had allowed Hitler to take over Germany, and I felt that as part of the country I, too, was responsible. But the main factor was that in the previous six years I had learnt something about following and trusting the inner leading of the Spirit, and so the certainty came that this was the right decision for me. Once I had decided I had no further doubt about it, and all that I had learnt in these experimenting years was to be of crucial value during my years in the army.

Chapter 8   1944

RETURNING in 1944 I was struck again by what a red-brick, new-looking place Fleetwood was, without many trees. But there were three glorious things about it which I rejoiced in – the seashore with the pools of water reflecting the breakwater, the colour of the sand and the pebbles. Then there were the sunsets, which seem to me even now more varied and delightful than any I have seen anywhere else in the world. And finally the view across Morecambe Bay, which on a clear day gave a panoramic view of the whole range of the Lakeland hills. This was particularly spectacular when the more distant ones were covered in snow.

I had always longed to find a way to express what I felt about these things. I had tried to do it in poetry, but wasn't very successful. It was only later that I found that I could express something of what I felt in painting. One of my paintings, which I have never put up for sale, was done along the coast there about 35 years ago. I was walking along the sea wall that extends to the west of the town along the sandhills – the area used to be the shooting range and is now the golf course. There were no houses for several miles. It's the wildest and most unspoilt spot on that coast and a favourite place for skylarks. On this particular November day everything was grey. The sea was grey. The sky was grey. Even the atmosphere felt grey. It was the kind of day when you feel there will never be any colour again in the world.

As I walked along the sea wall, suddenly the clouds began to open, and it was as if the world was seeing a new gentle dawn. The sand which had seemed dull became a reddish golden colour, the pebbles a lovely blue grey, and the sky a delicate tint of very light blue and pale gold with a touch of red in the clouds at the horizon, as it was towards evening.

By chance or by habit, I had my paints with me, and I quickly went below the sea wall on to the pebbles, took out my pad and put down in rapid and simple strokes what I saw and what I felt. The light lasted about half an hour, but that was all I needed. It was one of those rare occasions as a painter when I felt that at least something of the wonder and delicacy of the moment had been captured. I had to do very little to it when I got home, and it has stayed on the walls of our various homes ever since. The thousand and more paintings which have been hung there and then sold have expressed something of what I feel, but this one and a handful of others have stayed because in their very simplicity they speak of the wonder of light in this country of ours. It is reproduced as *Plate No 2: Evening light, Fleetwood* (facing page 86).

One of the first things I did after being with my family was to get on a train and go up to Grasmere to see my old friends, Heaton Cooper and his wife Ophelia. Heaton was, and still is at 90, one of the most prominent of the Lakeland artists.

Arriving in Grasmere I went to the studio and found that they were staying over near Crummock Water. I telephoned them to be told, 'At the back of the studio you'll find a bike, get on it and come over immediately.' After two hours' hard cycling I arrived at the Kirkstile Inn and was told to go down to the lakeside. So in one of the most beautiful spots in the world we were reunited. I had brought some fresh Fleetwood fish from my mother and having had a warm embrace from Ophelia, I presented it to her. 'I thought there was a funny smell when I kissed you,' she said.

Over the years the Lakeland hills had drawn me more and more. Every Easter from when I was about 11 my mother, father, sister and I used to go up and stay at the Methodist Guild house, Abbott Hall, at Kents Bank on the other side of Morecambe Bay. From there each day we would traverse the short distance to the lakes themselves. I remember being very struck that every single one of those hills, or fells as I learnt to call them, even the crags, had their own names. I think I was about 12 when I did my first climb, up Helvellyn. Even though there was a thick mist on the top and I couldn't see anything, it was exhilarating. I don't think I've ever lost the sheer delight of getting on top of a mountain.

When I was 17 I met Heaton Cooper at an Oxford Group gathering, and our friendship has lasted over these 59 years. I remember feeling very proud that I could call a famous artist my friend. I used to look at his paintings, especially one of the evening light on Pillar Rock, and marvel at the glory of it. I didn't dream at that point of ever being able to express myself in anything like that way, but gradually it became an aspiration to master the technique necessary to put on paper my deepest feelings and emotions.

People sometimes say to me, 'Oh, aren't you lucky to have such a gift!' I say, 'Yes, I am, but whatever gift I have is 30 per cent gift and 70 per cent hard work and discipline in learning the skills.'

I think that there exists in all human beings a sense of wonder at the world around: the seas, the mountains, the trees, and the animals and people. And for each there may well be a way, undiscovered as yet, in which that wonder can be conveyed. It can be in painting, in sculpture, in music, in poetry, or in prose, in a novel or a play, but also in carpentry, building or creating a home. Perhaps the important thing is to find the gift and to spend the time and thought in developing whatever particular latent talent is there.

Cardinal Hume writes, 'Beauty is one of the means by which we are led to God. It is the beautiful which can arouse in us "wonder".'

Chapter 9   LONDON AND
'THE FORGOTTEN FACTOR'

MY NEXT step after Fleetwood and the Lake District was to go to London and meet the people who were carrying on the work of MRA there. They were few, as most had gone into the armed forces. One or two of them I knew, but my touch with the Oxford Group before the war had been quite a slight one, even though the things I had learnt from people who had met the Group had played such an important part in my life.

At the same time I had to report to the army for duty. The conviction had grown in me that I should get into a part of the army where I could have some part in training people for peacetime. So I suggested that they should post me to the Army Education Corps. The senior officers interviewing me for the posting looked very doubtful: you had to have a university degree to be eligible, and I'd left school with a very ordinary school certificate; you had to be over 30 years of age, and I was 26; you also had to be below category A in health, and although I'd lost the sight of my right eye, I was still in Grade A. However my conviction was strong, and their flexibility was admirable: so after some consideration I was transferred from the artillery to the Education Corps.

It started with a period in London when I was able to stay at the MRA headquarters. This was most valuable training in MRA and its objectives, and afforded the opportunity to learn all that had happened during the war years.

I was then posted to be on the staff of the Army Education School at Wakefield. Because I'd had some training in accountancy, I was given the task of training shorthand typists to teach their subject to the troops. Someone said rather cynically, 'We, who are not teachers, are training people who don't want to teach to teach people who don't want to learn.'

All the same I enjoyed it, but the important new development at this time, which became a factor in the pattern of my life, was my feeling that I should get to know people in the mining industry. So along with friends working with MRA in the area, we got to know some of the miners in Doncaster.

About this time Frank Buchman, the initiator of the Oxford Group who was then instigating its development into the campaign for moral and spiritual re-armament, arrived back in Britain. He came from America with a group who were presenting Alan Thornhill's play about people in industry, *The Forgotten Factor*.

We took our miner friends down to London to see the play. They met Frank Buchman and told him, 'This play must come to the coalfields of Yorkshire. It is just what we need.' Frank's response was enthusiastic, and shortly afterwards, just at the time I was leaving the army, I found myself helping to organise performances of this play to packed audiences in Doncaster and in the mining communities around. The play had a startling effect on audiences, nearly all miners and their wives, and led to quite a new spirit in many pits. I had no idea at the time that theatre was to play such a major part in my life.

The decision to abandon the job waiting for me in the Treasury Department of the Lancashire County Council was not a difficult one. Although it was safe and sure and might have led to a good career, after what I'd seen and been through I felt I wanted to devote myself to something that might move directly to bring the change in the world so desperately needed.

So in June 1946 I decided instead to work with the people of MRA, fully realising that no one was paid a salary and that I would have to rely on my own faith, work, and initiative to have enough to live on. At that age it didn't concern me very much. Many others from the services, most of whom also had no private means, also decided to do this.

At this point I was in the midst of what had become a major campaign in the coalfields with *The Forgotten Factor*. After a tour of the coalfields the play went on to a run at the Westminster Theatre, which had just been bought as a memorial to men and women of MRA who had been killed in the war, and we took miners down to London who would speak before the performances.

It was a fairly busy life and a fascinating one, but I was having difficulties with my stomach, and the doctors pointed out that I'd never really relaxed since my escape. They advised me to take a long break. I was very reluctant to do so, but I did agree and arranged to stay for many weeks in Baysbrown, a lonely farm house in the Lake District, near my two painter friends Heaton Cooper and Bernard Eyre-Walker. This was one of those unplanned incidents that was very important for the future, for as a result painting became a major part of my life.

Bullcroft Colliery   Photo: P Sisam

After touring the mining areas, 'The Forgotten Factor' came to the Westminster Theatre and attracted large delegations of miners

95

Chapter 10   THE LANGDALE VALLEY

EACH DAY, during that winter of 1947, I would go out with either Bernard or Heaton, who lived in the next valley of Grasmere, and watch them at work. Then I would make my own attempts, and they would be very generous in giving time and thought to me.

These two men had very different approaches to their painting. Bernard, a gentle and philosophical man, would approach a subject with the feeling that it was so wonderful that he couldn't possibly express it in a painting. He would be almost in awe of it. Also he would be very meticulous in finding just the right position from which to tackle it. I've known him to walk round for an hour in order to find the appropriate foreground and to wait for the light and sky to match the subject.

His paintings are therefore very sensitive. He was also colour blind in reds, and so his work came over with rather subdued colours but with great delicacy of feeling. He used to say to me, 'Don't paint until there is something you really want to say, something you must say. It's no good just painting a scene. If there is something before you – the light on the fells, the reflections in a lake, or the windswept clouds, whatever it is that strikes you, say that.'

I also learnt from him that if you sit down to try and capture the particular aspect which caught your attention, you should stick to that. Then if, whilst painting, something else strikes you (as it nearly always will) don't put that in as well, or you will generally end up by spoiling or neutralising your principle point.

Despite this perfectionist attitude, he would sometimes say, 'There is nothing particularly wonderful about the light today, but let's go down to the other end of Elterwater where the Brathay comes out of the lake. There is always something to paint there.' And there nearly always was.

Heaton, on the other hand, would be so excited by what he saw that he would sit down at the earliest moment and with great strokes of bold colour make his statement. His mastery of the medium and his skill in letting the water-colour flow were such that he generally succeeded in a very short time. I've heard him say that at certain points in his life he would do as many as six or seven paintings in a day.

He also became so popular that he said to me once, 'The trouble is that I can sell almost anything I paint.' His paintings too have very much reflected his own state of mind and spirit, sometimes becoming rather stylised whilst at other times expressing his own inner search for truth.

Later in our lives, I urged him to tell the story of his life and painting. After initial doubts ('Who would be interested?'), he did produce what I believe is his finest work, *Mountain Painter*, which he very generously dedicated to me. It tells his story and is illustrated by a great number of colour plates.

This stay in the Langdale Valley was rich in many different ways. First of all I learnt a great deal from these two men about technique, how to put on a wash, how to deal with that most fascinating subject, water.

I think it was there that I realised for the first time that in painting water you have to capture four different aspects. First there are the reflections when the water is still. Then the reflection of the colours of the sky in ruffled water. With the water's edge nearest to you, you can see the pebbles beneath it. And finally the shadows thrown on the water surface by a tree or a rock. I learnt from my friends the several different ways of trying to convey this complex subject. *(Plate no 4: facing page 87)*

There were many simple lessons to be learnt, such as not disturbing a wash until it was dry, which was always difficult for someone as impatient as I am. It's hard to wait for the wash to dry before putting the next one on, especially as the light is changing constantly on the subject you are looking at. And in those winter months with not much warmth in the sun, the paint sometimes took a long time to dry. In addition there was the hazard of the water freezing as you got higher up on the fells. These were all the delights and difficulties of painting in what the Impressionists called *plein air*.

I also learnt from my friends something you won't find in most text books – how to make use of your mistakes. What to do with an uneven wash in the sky. Can it be turned into a cloud effect? How to take colour out, for instance on a lake where in the distance there is a line of ruffled water. How to avoid muddiness. And to learn by patiently watching, asking, and experimenting, which pigments to use to get the shades you want. Bernard taught me to start off with just eight or nine pigments, and when I had mastered them to expand my palette further. I was amazed at how many different shades it is possible to get from a limited range. I also learnt to look at the sky and the shadows of the day, and to decide which basic blue to use – cobalt, ultramarine or Windsor blue, and the advantage of sticking to that blue in the shadows throughout the painting.

Having eventually mastered these rules, it is possible to break them in order to get particular effects. I could go on and on – the use of a razor blade when painting a ruffled surface of a stream, the need to watch the flow of a stream and get its rhythm rather than trying to paint each little movement, but above all to watch, and watch, then watch again. *(Plate no 5: facing page 150)*

That winter the snow lay thick on the fells for many weeks. For the hill farmers it was very difficult, as they had to climb up in the deep snow and often dig the sheep out when they were completely buried in the drifts. In fact many sheep, even of the tough Herdwick breed, were lost.

From a painter's view, it was glorious. Covered by snow, the mountains' shapes were wonderfully revealed, undistracted by the colours of the fells. I fell in love with snow landscapes, with the freshness and clarity of the shadows from the deep cobalt or purple in the foreground to the delicate blues in the distance.

I remember painting a snow scene in Switzerland which I gave to a good friend. I felt that in some ways it portrayed absolute purity. Understanding purity has been for me a journey. Growing up with the idea that anything to do with sex was dirty, I had slowly to realise that sex was holy, one of the many gifts of God which he can give or withhold – and that both the giving and withholding are gifts – and that there are many other aspects to purity.

Bernard and Heaton were so different in temperament that although they sometimes went out to paint together, they seldom chose the same subject; so a joint expedition hardly ever worked out, and they would generally end up in different parts of the fells and make their own way home without meeting up again.

Both men were a great encouragement in every way and especially regarding these first serious attempts of mine at water-colour. I have several of these earlier sketches still in my store and have based on them several paintings which I completed recently.

I remember especially one occasion from that period when Bernard had taken me with him in his car to spend a few days in Wasdale. It had poured with rain each day, and we had only managed one brief time in which we could sketch. The day we were due to leave was more promising, so I said to Bernard that I would like to walk back to the Langdale Valley rather than going with him by car.

I climbed up out of Wasdale up to Sty Head Tarn and then up the steep rise to Sprinkling Tarn, which lies under the shadow of Great End. The day was clear and bright. It is a good long walk, largely high up, and in the midst of the most lovely and spectacular of the Lakeland fells, with Sca Fell, Esk Pike and Bow Fell on one side and Glaramara on the other, with several deep ravines including the one leading to the Langstrath valley dipping down towards Borrowdale. The ground up there seemed to have a springiness in it, and the air was clear, and as I walked along the rough path, I remember feeling this sense of there being another dimension beyond the world as we know it. It's a sensation I've had only on rare occasions, and this walk on that February day is one of the most vivid.

I don't remember meeting any one at all until after I had passed Angle Tarn and Rossett Ghyll. I dropped down into the Langdale Valley and in the evening light arrived back at Baysbrown Farm for a very welcome evening meal.

Many years later I did a painting looking back from the ridge towards Great Gable. This was on a misty day when my wife, Mary, and I had climbed up to Sprinkling Tarn hoping to paint there, but finding it very dark and dull, we went on above the tarn to the ridge overlooking the Sty Head Pass. Suddenly Great Gable appeared, clothed in a delicate misty light, so I had to sit down immediately to try to capture that moment. (*Plate no 2: facing page 55*)

Years later I did a series of paintings based on a phrase in Psalm 104 'clothed in light' – one of them was derived from this painting which Heaton Cooper bought from me and which he still has in his house in Grasmere. (*Plate no 6: facing page 151*)

From this time was born a very deep love of the Lakeland fells, which was deepened when I discovered

100

that my grandmother's family came from the southern part of Lakeland. She and her husband had been married at Cartmel Priory, and my grandfather had been a stone mason who had carved some of the statues in the Whitehaven church.

Chapter 11 AMERICA – AND MARRIAGE

AFTER this time in the Lake District I had a very generous invitation from some American MRA friends to spend some time over there. They felt it would be both good experience, and also that with good food away from the rationing in Britain I would regain strength.

In the end I stayed three years. I found myself touring with plays and musicals, often speaking to clubs and gatherings and also involved with training young people. I learnt a lot. I also met there, in Los Angeles, the wonderful girl who was to become my wife. She was English, from a landowning family, who had been working in a factory in Birmingham during the war and had contracted TB. She, like myself, had been invited to work with MRA in America.

At first Mary was just one of many delightful younger people there drawn from many countries. Then something happened. A colleague and I who were taking some responsibility for the work received a telegram from our friends in San Francisco, where they were presenting a play, asking for more people to go and help them and mentioning amongst others, Mary Evans. We were at a party at the time. I was going up on the overnight train, and after a brief consultation we decided that Mary couldn't really be spared. When I got back a few weeks later this 'quiet English girl' said to me, with flames shooting out of her eyes, 'How dare you decide what I should do and without even mentioning the invitation to me, and then you go up there yourself!' I began to get a very different idea of this 'quiet English girl'.

Whenever I tell about this incident she will add, 'Yes, and I still haven't been to San Francisco.'

It was shortly after this when the completely unexpected thought came into my mind, when I was having a time of quiet, 'One day you will marry Mary Evans.' It was a surprise because I had in mind a short list of girls whom I thought I would like to marry, and Mary wasn't one of them. They were girls whom I thought were possibly more dynamic – I discovered later how wrong I was.

103

After this, I began to look out for her amongst the hundred, mostly young people, in the MRA Centre there who were putting on the big musical *The Good Road* aimed at giving new values to Hollywood.

I remember how much I liked the yellow-gold dress she sometimes wore in the evening and also the checked cotton dress which made her look so young and vulnerable. If we had a party visiting friends or going to Santa Monica for a swim, I discovered I was particularly pleased if Mary was one of them.

As I saw more of her during the next weeks, quietly serving at table or out meeting all kinds of people, I noticed how she gave herself in uncalculating friendship

Mary at the MRA centre in Los Angeles

Mary with father, mother, sisters and brother-in-law outside Buckingham Palace

to everyone no matter who they were. I realised that she was a very special person and gradually I knew I was falling in love with her. However, I didn't feel that the time was ripe to tell her what I felt. God knew what was going on in her heart and would tell me the right time to propose.

As it worked out, Mary and I were in different parts of the world for the next year or two, heavily involved in different campaigns. Sometimes I wavered from the idea of Mary. I remember one time when a young Swiss student came to work with us and I became infatuated with her. One day the thought came to me, 'She is not the one for you', and the infatuation just disappeared like mist when the sun comes up. So much for the current belief, 'I'm in love – I can't do anything about it.'

Mary joined us in Italy in 1952 to help with putting on Alan Thornhill's play *The Forgotten Factor* in Italian. It became clear to me that she was meant to be my life partner.

I used to dream of how I would propose to her on the bridge over the stream in the grounds of her home at Whitbourne, which I had previously visited, or in some equally romantic setting. Actually, I went over to Birmingham and proposed in the sitting room of the friends she was staying with – but it was an even more romantic moment than I had dreamt of. I really didn't know what she felt. I was over the moon when she gave a wholehearted 'yes', and told me that since those days in California she had been in love with me.

The following day we took the bus to her home in Herefordshire, talking about our future but we kept breaking into Italian to say what we felt – *carissima* or *bellissima* are much more expressive in Italian than English, and also we thought that probably the other people in the bus wouldn't understand.

We were married on June 13th that year on a beautiful day in the lovely eleventh century church at Whitbourne in Herefordshire with the reception at her family home, Whitbourne Hall.

At the beginning of our marriage I think it is true to say that I was the dominant partner, but gradually I learnt that Mary's insight was something I needed and if I didn't stop and listen I should regret it. I also realised that Mary made many more lasting friendships than I did and that I had much to learn from her in that.

So often when I've been engaged in some project which I've been determined to carry through she has sensed that

Outside the Church

Outside Whitbourne Hall, Mary's family home, with our parents

all was not well, and has taught me to stop and look again at what I am doing and my motives. I believe that God put us together for His purposes and for our joy.

Our growing together has developed in so many different ways. I had discovered before we were married that we both loved walking in the countryside or in the mountains. What I hadn't known was how different we were in the things we noticed.

I would be walking along entranced with the formation of clouds, the light on the hills or the shape of trees, when Mary would say, 'Oh there's a greenfinch. I haven't seen one of those around here before,' or suddenly spot some flower hiding in the hedgerow. I'm still amazed how she can see these minute and enchanting things whilst walking along. What has happened of course is that she has become more aware of landscape, shapes, and sky, and I have learnt to love and appreciate flowers and birds and small plants.

In our earlier years, whilst I painted, Mary would climb the nearest mountain top and this only stopped about eight years ago. I was painting near the side of the road leading towards Crummock Water (a spectacular view) and for practically the first time I had finished my painting before she reappeared. It's the only time I've been worried and wondered if I should call out the Mountain Rescue people. There was no one else on the fells that evening. Before I could do that, however, I spotted her coming down the snow-covered slopes of Grasmoor, soaking wet having slithered down the snow in order to find her way back. Since then she has taken up photography! She has a very good eye for taking a picture, and they are really splendid.

Our backgrounds also show up in our attitude to aches and pains. If I have something wrong I say so – sometimes too soon and too often. Mary's tradition is that you must not mention aches and pains unless they are at the stage where you must have a doctor (or an undertaker), and even then you must underplay it. I've discovered this is a common trait in all her family, with some of the spouses complaining that they never know what is going on. Again Mary has become more willing (sometimes after cross-questioning) to admit that she isn't well. Equally I think I have learnt not to squeal and moan at every discomfort.

Another area where we have grown together is in our approach to our Christian faith. Mary was brought up as an Anglo-Catholic and so views faith from the perspective of the Church holding the truth of the faith for humanity. My upbringing has been more in the Nonconformist tradition of Tyndale and Bunyan, believing that each person was responsible through the Bible for finding his own way to God. Of course both are true and can and should be means of growing in our understanding of God and of our own lives.

Mary manages to combine being a traditional wife and homemaker, looking after laundry, meals and home, with being decidedly her own person with her own conviction and calling. This was exemplified some seven years ago when we saw on TV the riots on Broadwater Farm when a policeman was murdered. She had the strongest feeling that she should get to know the leader of the community, Dolly Kiffin. For two or three months she talked about it and tried to get an introduction to her. Finally through her friend Betty Rainbow, they got an introduction and went across London to meet her and make friends with her.

This friendship led to Dolly coming to the MRA centres at Tirley Garth in the north of England and to Caux in Switzerland. All this has helped her to bring quite a transformation to that troubled estate. Mary and Betty have taken that journey by tube scores of times in the last seven years and have helped her to write her own life story which has just been published. This is just one illustration of the combination of being a traditional homemaker and having an individual life's calling.

Another instance concerns Burma. After the war ended Mary's mother and father had a visit from someone who had served with her brother John in the frontier service in Burma. John had been cut off there when the Japanese invaded and had escaped into China where he led a band of guerrilla fighters. He was eventually killed during a raid into Burma.

This colleague of his told Mary's parents that he thought they should know that John had formed a relationship with a beautiful Shan girl and that they had had a daughter. Mary's parents, with their background, were rather naturally shocked by this news and were not keen to talk about it. In fact Mary only found out some years later, and then she and her sister Gwen set out to try and find John's daughter. This they did quite quickly through some Burmese friends.

This girl, whose name is Nang Hom, was by then about 14 years of age and had been brought up by the widow of

108

the ruler of the province (Kengtung) in the Shan States. John had been very helpful to them when the ruler had been assassinated, and so she had generously taken in Nang Hom and her mother and looked after them when John was killed. Mary started to write and got wonderful letters back in schoolgirl English; this was followed by sending Nang Hom parcels and photographs, a correspondence that continued for 20 years.

It wasn't possible in those years to visit that part of Burma – inside the Golden Triangle – but in 1986, when Nang Hom and her husband and children had moved to another part of the Shan States, Mary with her brother Robin took an adventurous journey to see her. After an overnight train ride from Rangoon and five hours in the back of a 'bus' (a truck with side seats in it), they had a wonderful meeting with their niece.

Since then, Burma has been an area of the world Mary has taken a great interest in, meeting with Burmese here in the UK and trying to get permission – unsuccessfully so far – for Nang Hom or some of her family to visit England.

In no other aspect of life have I been so grateful for the leading of the Holy Spirit as in our marriage. I think that one essential ingredient lies in the fact that we were both individually committed to trying to find God's will and do it. When times have been difficult, and these occurred from time to time especially in our early life together, we would stop and seek together for the direction of the Holy Spirit.

We have come to regard difficulties, not as disasters, but as something the good Lord has allowed so that we can learn from them, change and grow. In fact that seems to be one very good reason for putting us together, so that two very imperfect characters could have the chance to develop.

In the 40 years we've been married we've become more in love and developed a greater relish for life all the time. If Mary has been away for a day or two or even a few hours, I am so excited and delighted that she is back. This, to us, is a wonder, and I was glad to have a letter the other day from our best man, Will Kneale. 'You have truly a marvellous wife', he wrote, '. . . I assisted at your wedding 40 years ago, and was as close to you as could be at that time. . . . Yet who could have visualised what you were to grow into together and create in your home and far beyond its walls. We had a glimpse of this at your ruby wedding celebration.'

I like Robert Louis Stevenson's poem:

> Trusty, dusky, vivid true
> With eyes of gold and bramble-dew
> Steel true and blade straight
> The great artifice
> Made my mate.
>
> Honour, anger, valour, fire
> A love that could never tire
> Death quench or evil stir
> The mighty master
> Gave to her.
>
> Teacher, tender, comrade wife
> A fellow-farer true through life
> Heart-whole and soul-free
> The august father
> Gave to me.

We are very ordinary people with all the imperfections of our human nature. We are also very privileged people – privileged to learn from a wide range of friends.

Some of the guests at our 40th wedding aniversary celebration

Chapter 12   ITALY

Six and a half years after my escape I was crossing the Italian frontier again. It was in the dark days of 1950, and Italy had just come through a civil war. Especially in the north, people had been tortured and shot by the fanatical minority of Fascists who carried on to the end. Then the tables had been turned; partisans had occupied the towns and strung up Mussolini and his mistress in Piazza Loreto in Milan, then taken their revenge on many who had collaborated with the old regime. In many places there was hardly a family who had not had someone killed in this civil war, and the ferment of bitterness and fear that remained made it very doubtful as to whether Italy would remain free or whether the Red dictatorship, which was already imposing its will on many towns and communities, would take over the whole country. This time I was going to Italy as a free man and not a hunted one, and to a free country. An atmosphere of intense fear and hatred at times seemed to dominate the country just as completely as an army of occupation. Despite this I was very glad to be going back. There was also the chance to try and repay the debt to those Italians who had risked their lives for me.

That summer I had come back to Europe from America to attend the Moral Re-Armament conference taking place at Caux in Switzerland. Caux in those post-war years seemed like a dream world to the thousands who poured in from Germany, France, Austria and Italy. Here, in one of the most beautiful spots in the world, a thousand people from every race and class and kind spent time under the same roof planning to create something new in the world, and they were enjoying it. The verve and the music and the plays which were being created there seemed like a new renaissance.

At the time I arrived, the first groups of Italian workers came to Caux from Sesto San Giovanni, known as Little Stalingrad, from Legnano, from Bologna, from Genoa and from Milan. These Italian workers had been brought up under Fascism and had lived through war, defeat, and then civil war. Then there had been four years with poverty and hunger always just round the corner; now they were suddenly pitched into a world where they were welcomed as honoured guests, where people of other nations cared enough to serve them at table, and where an international chorus of British, French, German and Americans sang to them songs in their own beloved Italian. It was almost unbelievable.

The Italians' stay in Caux was generally only for three or four days. It was really much too short a time. Only after 48 hours did they really begin to understand the implications of all they were seeing. This wasn't just a marvellous gathering, but a determined attempt to alter things in the world, and they would be invited to play their part and to start by putting right the things which were wrong in their own lives. Their third day was often quite a turbulent one, as they argued with themselves – and being Italians they didn't keep what they thought to themselves. For most it was a question of whether they were going to return to the old choruses, 'You can't change the bosses.' 'They were at fault.' 'They were to blame, and they must change first,' or to accept their own responsibility. Many did decide right there and then. Others decided later. We didn't know what the permanent effect would be.

However, the fact that they were there at all was something of a marvel. It had happened because an Italian princess and a countess had read about Caux and one day had just turned up there, eager to help. A ten days' stay had permanently affected their lives, and on their return to Milan they had invited the leading industrial figures of the country to dinner and over coffee had so portrayed Caux for them that two weekends later they all arrived there themselves. Caux stirred them up too. Some saw hope for the first time of ending the class struggle in Italy, and so they sent these delegations of workers and managers from their factories, together, to Caux. Some were affected in their own ideas and lives; some left and never came back.

A few weeks after all this, invited by some of the leading Italians, seven of us who knew a little of Italy and the language, had packed our bags and taken what little money we had and crossed the frontier from Switzerland to Italy. The party included Leslie Fox, a chartered accountant who had worked in Italy for his firm, Frank Romer, who had served in the British Army in Italy, and Adam McLean, who had been wounded whilst fighting with the US Army in Italy and had made great friends with many Italians in Rome. Adam, Leslie, and I made our way to Sesto San Giovanni. The town was then held

112

The Caux Conference Centre

Photo: Mike Blundell

Italians in the crowded meeting hall with, in left foreground, Princess Castelbarco

Dr Costa, President of Confindustria, with other members of his executive

113

by the Communists, and there were few who dared speak up against them. We got off the electric tram from Milan, and it really seemed as if we were in occupied territory again – we were being watched by everyone. I don't think anyone knew who we were, but we were strangers, probably foreigners, and somehow enemies. Our goal was the house of one of the Italian Communist workers we had met at Caux, and we split up and watched first to see if we were being followed, before making our way to his house. The welcome was overwhelming. He had been to Caux, but now he was wondering whether Caux had been a dream, and there we were at his front door. We called on several of these men, and always there was the same welcome.

As we had nowhere to sleep and not enough money to stay in a hotel, we asked at each home whether they could put one of us up, and so I found myself sleeping in the attic room of the 15 year old son of a man who had been the head of the works' council of a big steel plant at the time of the civil war. This man had seemed quiet at Caux, but now in his home and from the managers of the steel plant, we learnt the whole story. It was he who had led the workers at the time when two of the managers had been thrown into the steel furnaces alive.

On his return from Caux he had gone to the management and had broken down in tears like a child, as he asked their forgiveness for the wrong that had been done. Then returning home, he had, to the delight of his wife, returned to his Catholic faith, and his home had been united again. We heard many such stories, but we also soon realised that violence was still expected and planned for by a great many. One of our number found a machine-gun under his bed, another discovered that there was a cache of arms buried nearby. A great many people in Sesto believed that violence was the only way to gain justice.

They were exciting days and sometimes dangerous. They were also hard days. We ate at the cheapest restaurants. We slept a few nights here and a few there, and generally someone had to move out of their own bed to give us one. We would sometimes have lunch with a countess and then have hardly enough money to buy a simple supper of bread, eggs and milk. It was a cold and damp winter in Milan, and our small band would meet together in the corner of a cafe in the centre of Milan, feet wet and eyes heavy through lack of sleep and rest, and

114

with the black marketeers making their whispered deals at the next table. There we would plan our own next moves. None of us felt that God had deserted us, but we sometimes wondered why it needed to be so hard and rough.

I suppose it was only six months later that we realised why we had to go through such a rough time. By then some of these hard-core Communist revolutionaries had become our close friends. They said, 'Caux was marvellous. It was like a dream to us – a classless society, the new world. But, we said, it's Utopia. There, where there is enough food and comfort and lovely surroundings, it's possible to do right and to care, but faced with cold and hunger and overcrowding and fear and discrimination and unemployment, it is impossible. And then you came and you lived amongst us, not as saints, but as men who admitted your faults and who were often wrong, but who stuck to your determination to do God's will in spite of deprivation and cold and discomfort, and in spite of a lack of welcome from some who could have helped. Now we know that this is an idea that really works.'

And so, day by day, we trained these few men in the rudiments of the ideas of Caux. We met them early in the morning before work and listened together in order to try and find God's plan. We met their friends with them and cared for them together, visiting them in their homes. Every tram route in the area became familiar to us, as well as the towns around.

Our team was greatly strengthened in these early stages by the arrival of three stalwart young Swiss women – Lucie Perranoud, Claire Locher and Hanni Weidemann. Not only did they share the rigours of our life with great resilience but also they brought with them warm-hearted qualities and the gift of languages. They were all fluent in Italian.

It was at this stage that there came a very big improvement in our living conditions. Walking through the centre of Milan one day we encountered a *marchesa*, one of the Milan aristocracy who had been to Caux. She greeted us warmly and was delighted that we were in Milan. She asked where we were living, and as she grasped the uncertainty of our lives, 'of no fixed abode', and nowhere to meet she said, 'But I have a *palazzo* (a town house) in the centre of the city. It is very dilapidated and filthy and is going to be pulled down, but you could have it in the meantime.' Right away she took us to see this building with reception rooms and several wings – unbelievably

115

filthy and run down. However, we decided that one wing of it with half a dozen rooms could be made habitable. So we gratefully accepted her offer.

It was at this point that we were joined by three young Americans – Jerry von Teuber, whose family had previously been a land-owning aristocratic family in the Czech Republic; Herbie Allen, a very talented musician; and Bill Baumann, who had a lovely singing voice. These young men were later to make a considerable contribution, through their gifts, to our company, but their first task was to put on their oldest clothes and to clean the *palazzo*. It was so filthy that they had to use wire wool to get the layers of dirt off the floor boards.

After two weeks this wing was habitable. Various of our friends from the factories lent us furniture and Ian and Sheena Sciortino, who had just arrived to help, became the first host and hostess. It meant that there was a place for some to sleep, we could have simple meals there, and above all we had a place to meet and to welcome our friends. This meant a lot of our friends from the factories who had never before been entertained in a *palazzo* – but also many of the managers and nobility came. This was one more demonstration to our Communist friends of the practicality of the ideas of Caux.

All this led us to many adventures, and soon we found ourselves producing plays. The first one, *The Forgotten Factor*, shook Milan. Mary joined us to help with this play.

This was probably a turning point in our work. The Princess Castelbarco and the Countess Cicogna, whose visit to Caux had started the whole thing, had organised a production of the play in the heart of Milan. The play itself had a great impact. Equally stunning was the fact that the part of the boss in the play was played by Umberto Baldini, the Director of Personnel of Montecatini, the great chemical combine of Italy which had factories and mines all over the country. The man playing the other leading part was Angelo Pasetto, who had been the head of the Communist cell in the headquarters of the company in Milan.

An amusing part of the evening was that, as we had not charged for tickets, the Princess and the Countess stood at the one exit of the theatre on each side of the door holding out silver trays. I saw many of the audience reaching for their wallets as they realised that there would be a collection, and then when they saw who was at the door reach again for a larger note.

116

After this the work began to reach out to Florence, Genoa, Trieste, Bologna, and Rome. We met many of the leaders of Italy, amongst them that great statesman de Gasperi, who as Prime Minister gave such inspired leadership in those years. Giuseppe Saragat, the leader of the Social Democrats and later President of Italy, also became a friend.

In 1957 our son John was born. Mary went to England where he was born at a Birmingham hospital. John and Mary spent the first six months at her home at Whitbourne, and after the christening in the lovely church we all returned to Italy where John became a part of all we were doing.

We used plays and films, one written by Angelo Pasetto, others translated from English, and although our main work was with individuals, we realised that plays were a particularly effective way of reaching the Italian people.

When we were staying at Montecatini in Tuscany with Dr Buchman, there was a great furore in the press. An industrialist called Marinotti had closed a factory in Florence because it was not profitable without any consultation with the workers. La Pira, the Mayor of Florence and a leading figure in the Christian Democrat party, fomented a good bit of opposition to this, and as a result the government in Rome took away Marinotti's passport. Dr Buchman was always keen to try and deal with the immediate as well as the long term and felt we should meet Marinotti. This happened quite quickly through a Dutch industrialist, and when he heard what we were doing in Italian industry he invited us to take *The Forgotten Factor* to Torviscosa in Udine. There he had cleared land during the Mussolini era and developed a large area to grow the raw materials needed for his textiles. He had built a factory in the middle of it to manufacture artificial fabrics. Later he quarrelled with Mussolini and had to leave the country rapidly. Now, after the war, he was one of the leading industrialists of the country.

We accepted the invitation and went with the cast of *The Forgotten Factor* to Torviscosa, where we were guests of the company. It was a complete company town where everything – houses, schools, hospital and church – was owned by the company. When Marinotti came, the flag was put up in the central square, and all was spruced up for his visit. They had a large theatre in the centre, and on the Saturday night it was packed to the roof with some 1,500 of the factory and agricultural workers. Marinotti duly

117

arrived from his headquarters in Milan, with all his entourage, and was delighted with the play and the response of his people. At the end he said, 'Have you got another play?' 'Yes, it's called *The Boss*.' 'Can you put it on next weekend?' So we said we would. To do this we had to enlist his head of personnel, who was a good amateur actor, and raise the rest of the cast and rehearse them hour after hour during the coming week. We had not told Marinotti that the central theme of the play was about a boss who had closed a factory without consulting the workers, and of the subsequent change in him.

Duly on the Saturday he arrived with all his staff. I was sitting just behind him, and as the play developed it was like watching a whale with a harpoon in it – he squirmed from side to side while his sycophantic staff muttered supporting words. At the end Angelo Pasetto, who had become quite close to Marinotti, stepped forward. Immediately Marinotti shouted to him, 'How are you going to make this work in practice?' Pasetto asked him to join him up on stage, and we witnessed what seemed like a final act of the play before 1,500 enthralled workers as they argued it out.

After the performance we thought, 'Well, that is the end of our association with Marinotti.' But apparently he didn't sleep well that night, and the next morning he called for us, and asked us if we would continue our work in his factories. In each place we had tried to build a nucleus of people who would accept change in their own lives and then apply it in their situation, and this we did in Torviscosa.

Perhaps our most startling success was in Sesto San Giovanni, the town near Milan known as Little Stalingrad, into which we had crept in those first weeks in Italy. We were invited by the head of the chemical workers of Italy to take two plays there, *The Vanishing Island* and an African play, *Freedom*. We presented them in the best hall in the town, and it was packed every night. The Communist mayor and many councillors came, and eventually the mayor gave a reception in the large hall of the Communist Party headquarters so that people could hear about Moral Re-Armament. This packed audience did respond to a wide range of speakers; workers, industrialists, trades union leaders, and people from Africa, Asia, and America.

One leading industrialist reckoned that the Communist take-over of Italy had been put back several years by what we did. I don't know whether this was true or not. I'm

118

'The Forgotten Factor' with Angelo Pasetto, Lelio Griselli, Paolo Marchetti, Commendatore Baldini and Mariella Zipponi

The Torviscosa complex

conscious of the many mistakes we made. Although our team grew to include Americans, French, Swiss and Austrians, I think we often tried to suggest that the pattern of life which we had adoptedwas something that the Italians should adopt; we didn't give enough freedom for them to find their own pattern. All I can say is that we tried to be obedient to the leading of the Holy Spirit and lives were changed.

It was a time of personal growth. In the midst of all this activity I sometimes felt a dullness and deadness in my life. I was vaguely aware that all was not well in my relationship with the colleague I was working with. But this was only brought home to me when a very good friend said quite forcibly that he thought I was 'dead from the feet up'. Soon I realised that I reacted strongly to my colleague whenever I didn't get appreciation and that that had caused the deadness. But then I had to go deeper and realise that my passion to be thought highly of ran my life and turned to bitterness when I didn't get appreciation.

I had to face the fact that my relationships had gone badly wrong and I was hurting those I loved most, and especially Mary. I began to realise that I had never uncovered the deepest drives of my life. It needed this shock treatment to make me aware of my nature – everybody else was only too aware.

Although I had been in Christian work for many years, I had never faced up to these things nor let Christ come in and heal, alter and cleanse. I discovered I was a prisoner to this just as much as I had been a prisoner in the physical sense during the war. It was a very great shock to realise this, and to face it and to turn to Christ, whom I had learned to trust, to cleanse and transform this inner core of my nature. When I did this, with great sorrow for the hurt it had caused, especially to those I loved most, there came a sense of cleansing and of feeling smaller and freer. I remember crying for the first time since my childhood.

This experience of repentance and forgiveness was the turning point in my Christian life. I believe that this failure to let Christ deal with our human nature at its deepest points is the reason why so many of us Christians are ineffective.

This is the most painful discovery of all, when you realise how wrong and selfish your motives are for doing even the best things. Our grandparents called it an 'experience of the Cross', and that is an apt description. The process goes on throughout life, but the pain of discovering 'wrong' yet again in ourselves is countered by the ever more certain knowledge of God's love and forgiveness, so that the discovery of previously unrecognised sin becomes also a cause for rejoicing in the grace of God. Gradually I learnt not to send out the cavalry squadrons of defence every time I felt the citadel of self was in danger, but to welcome further liberation.

During these years we took many of our Italian friends to conferences in the USA, Switzerland, and Britain. Because of the dramatic circumstances and the flair of the Italians, they always made a great impact. I think we became rather pleased with ourselves. At a certain point we realised that we needed to take stock and look at our work in Italy, and also individually to be sure what our calling was. For me it meant venturing into new fields.

Whatever our shortcomings I believe we did affect people's lives, and personally I was grateful for the chance to try and repay the debt I owed to the Italian people, some of whom had risked their lives for me.

During these years with this big campaign in the northern cities of Italy, the mountains of the Abruzzi seemed far away. Now I felt I had neglected my friends Vittorio, Anna and Elisa Massara and I must try to go and see them. It was almost twenty years since I'd been hidden and helped by them.

TWENTY YEARS LATER

I wrote in my diary after my visit:

'The train from Sulmona to L'Aquila stopped at the little station right there in the fields by the river. I could see the village up there on the mountainside looking as grey and distant as ever. The walk up took longer than I thought – two and a half miles uphill seems longer when you are nearly 50. The village was very quiet, no one around at all. It was Sunday morning, and they were probably all at Mass. I found Vittorio and Anna's house without any difficulty; after all, the village was only 17 houses on each side of a single track. The house had been largely rebuilt and looked neat and new. An old lady came up the track. I asked her if Vittorio and Anna were at home. "No", she said in the local dialect, "They are at their daughter's in L'Aquila," but she didn't know the address.

'I went to the house opposite and wondered if I knew the people there. A girl in her thirties opened it, and I asked her, "Do you know the address of Vittorio and Anna's daughter at L'Aquila?" "Yes", she said, "But who are you?" I said, "I'm Rinaldo." She threw up her arms in the air, seized me, planted a kiss on both cheeks and shouted, "Mama, Papa c'e Rinaldo!" It seemed that the village began to vibrate. I said, "But who are you?" She said, "I'm Anna." Anna – the little girl of 12 who used to come with her sister and sit around the table with us as we cracked almonds.

'Soon mother and father were there, and I heard all the news and adventures of the last 22 years, but particularly the days after I had left when the village had been surrounded, and the Germans were trying to get us – after we had left.

'They gave me coffee and cake and pressed me to stay for lunch. But as the trains on to L'Aquila were few I told them I must go on – they understood. After all it was Vittorio and Anna who kept and sheltered me for three months.

'The little train came, and we wound along the valley bottom towards L'Aquila. Again the memories flooded in. This was the line where we looked for the signal box, and there was St Demetrio with his little *funavia* where we also looked for the box with a number. It had been a message over 'Clandestine Radio': "At so many miles, in such and such a direction from us in a named village, there would be a box number so and so, and there would be a parachutist to meet us." I had searched for that box but never found it. Perhaps it was a hoax because it had taken us right into the German supply line. But for us it had been our salvation for it was there we met Vittorio.

'The train wound slowly on, and we approached the Grand Sasso, that glorious snow-covered mountain, the highest of the Appennine chain, where we had had so many adventures.

'The train pulled into L'Aquila. It was one o'clock. I made my way to the address that Anna had given me. I found the entrance to the courtyard where they lived and on enquiring was shown the door up on the third balcony. I rang the bell. After a few minutes a little girl of about seven came. I knew at once I was in the right house; she looked just like Elisa had 22 years before. "Is your mama in?", I said, and in a moment a lady in her thirties appeared. I said, "It's Elisa, isn't it?" She looked and then, "Rinaldo, Rinaldo, Rinaldo", and like a long-lost brother I was welcomed home. She took me to the kitchen where the family were eating. Without saying who I was she showed me in. There was Vittorio, still the same Vittorio, a little greyer and older, but the same. He said in that most courteous manner of the Italian mountain folk, "Favourite – will you join us?" Elisa said, "It's Rinaldo." Anna, a little older and greyer, jumped up and kissed me on both cheeks, Vittorio too. Then they introduced me to Elisa's husband. I was home.

'They were in the middle of dinner, so quickly they moved, put on more food for me, so much that I nearly burst, and then the years rolled back and we re-lived again all the events that had bound our lives together. They told me, too, of the five other English soldiers whom they had sheltered for many weeks after I had left, one seriously wounded. And then, "You are the only one who ever wrote or remembered." I felt like the one leper in the ten who had come back to thank Christ – except that it was after 20 years.

'I must stay, I must cancel my plans, I must come back with my family, they said. Anyhow I stayed the night. In the morning Vittorio showed me the town. We walked through the streets together. After a while silently. I re-membered how he had asked me to help him emigrate. I had tried but failed to find the right thing. I wished now I had tried harder, although he had himself eventually found work in Venezuela and done quite well. Eventually I said, "I have always been sorry I couldn't help more to find you work." He waved his hand eloquently saying, "All that is past now." I said, "The only thing I did manage to find was that opportunity in Australia." He said, "Yes, but that would have involved too much money to get there." But he understood that I would have liked to have done more and understood how, in the travelling life I have lived, it had been difficult. I knew he understood, and I was glad and at peace. I said, "There are some debts one can never repay and this is one." He waved his arms again in a deprecating way. He knew that I meant it, and he knew that it was true.

'Next day we went back to "our village". All the old friends came to greet me. Anna made much of the fact that I had always written at Easter and Christmas, though in fact it was not even every year; and of the packages I sent, which were few. In the way of all ordinary folk she recounted every detail to the neighbours of my arrival the day before, and they all said, "You must come and stay." Then we went up to the terraced hillside and found the

123

"hole in the ground" where we had slept for two months, no longer covered with a roof of brushwood, but still there. I did a couple of sketches with my water colours which I had brought with me, and Vittorio fell asleep on the grass as he waited beside me.

'The time came to leave. We left the village, much altered now with running water and a rough road up to it. Many had gone or only came back at the weekends. Its people were still people of the heart, unintoxicated by materialism. As we walked down the hill I said a prayer to God that this quality would survive our present flood of heartlessness, and I prayed that we would find the ways of peace to draw out the greatness in people. I thought of the Germans who were then our enemies. They were now my friends. That was something of an advance.

'We said goodbye. The train pulled out of the station in the middle of the field. I was glad I had gone back. Life had been enriched by it, my life and theirs too.'

Vittorio Massara with grand-daughter, 1961

Chapter 13   SOUTH AMERICA

AFTER my time in Italy I had increased conviction that the presenting of God's truth through the arts of theatre and film was supremely important.

My father was very ill at this time. I was able to return home to spend the last days of his life with him. He was a man with a very real and deep faith. When the doctor told us that he wouldn't recover, we decided that he should be told this, so the doctor went up to his bedroom to tell him.

A little later I went to his bedroom, and he said, 'You know what the doctor said. He said, "Mr Mann, you are a good man, and I think you would like to know that you won't get up from your bed again".' I asked my father, 'Did this surprise you?' and he replied, 'You mean that he said I was a good man?', and laughed.

After my father died, Mary and I were invited to South America to help with the promotion of a Japanese play called *The Tiger*. It was almost a pageant and was drawing crowds of 10,000 or more, so it had had to move out of theatres into the football stadiums. We left our son, then aged four, to be looked after by a good friend, Kristin Squire. Mary stayed nine months, and I was there for 18 months.

When the company of *The Tiger* left I found myself staying on to help with the distribution of a film called *The Crowning Experience*, starring Muriel Smith, who had played the lead in *Carmen Jones* and then in *Carmen* with the Royal Opera Company in London. It was a musical based on the life of Mary McLeod Bethune, a pioneer in education for black people in the USA, and dealt movingly and trenchantly with colour prejudice. We were a small group left behind, but our conviction was to reach a million people every week. We decided that eight copies of the film, which had been excellently dubbed into Portuguese, should be circulated, and that it should be backed by TV programmes as well as newspaper articles in all the main papers.

At the time the agreement was signed with a distributor, I was staying with Colonel Pessoa – an air force officer who was often seconded to government to help expedite projects. I had gradually understood that the military in Brazil regarded themselves as the guardians of the country, ready to step into the political arena when things became too desperate. As they were thought of as being both patriotic and relatively free from corruption, they were often called in also by business leaders to handle many diverse tasks – even to the running of steel plants.

Over breakfast I told Colonel Pessoa that my colleague Frank McGee, who was handling the film distribution, and the rest of us, had a problem. The distributor wanted to launch all eight copies of *The Crowning Experience* in about four weeks' time. The copies were in Los Angeles and not only did we not have the money to fly them down, but also we didn't know whether we would eventually recoup the cost from our share of the box office receipts. It was clearly impractical to get the copies down in any other way.

After breakfast the Colonel said, 'Let's go out', and without saying what he was going to do, we drove to the air force base nearby, where he asked the sentry on duty who was in charge. Finding that the deputy commander was an old friend we went in to meet him.

After the usual embraces and introductions Colonel Pessoa said, 'My friend here, Mann, has a wonderful film that will do a great deal for Brazil. Distribution has been arranged, and the star of the film is the wonderful singer, Muriel Smith.' He then gave a vivid account of her career on Broadway and at Covent Garden in London, adding, 'She's a beautiful girl and we must get her down here.' Then, as an afterthought, 'Oh, and she has some baggage and material to bring down.' The deputy commander was impressed and got on the phone, but after a few calls gave up and said, 'Let's go and see the General.' After introductions he then told the story himself. It got better and better with the telling – and he didn't forget about the baggage. So then the General got on the phone and after a very short time said, 'That's alright, VARIG (the national airline) will give Muriel Smith a return ticket and will also give free transport to the "baggage".'

This was one of the delights of Brazil: they seemed to believe that anything was possible.

Having got the return ticket and free passage for the copies of the film, Colonel Pessoa decided we must now get together a worthy committee of invitation. So within a very short time an outstanding committee of about a

126

dozen nationally known figures had been formed. This included Marshall Dutra – whom you could call the Churchill of Brazil – and others representing government, military, industry and media, including the legendary figure Chateaubriand. He was the man who had been largely responsible for creating the Brazilian Air Force and was now the owner of *El Cruzeiro* (the *Life* magazine of South America), five television stations and many of the leading newspapers of the country.

So a telegram went off signed by those men inviting Muriel to come down for the launching of the film. She accepted, promising to arrive after finishing the film she was making.

So began a very extensive tour of the country, with interviews and recitals on TV and commercials (free) about

Muriel Smith

Photo: Weber, Luzern

the film several times a day. After the launching in Rio de Janeiro where we had put up (free) 10,000 posters, I realised that this wasn't enough – because at the end of the week a friend said to me, 'Oh, by the way, when is this film of yours being shown?' So when we launched it in Sao Paulo we got 30,000 posters up, as well as all the commercials.

Muriel was a great delight. Although often temperamental, she rose wonderfully to occasions. The one I remember most was at a big dinner reception in Rio de Janeiro organised by Chateaubriand. He himself was paralysed, but he instructed his editor in Rio to give a big reception for Muriel Smith. Everybody of importance in the city came. Muriel was sitting at the head table, and Frank McGee and I were at side tables. The atmosphere was one of great cynicism, and when the editor made a very cynical speech introducing her, I wondered what on earth Muriel would do and prayed hard for her.

She was a great perfectionist and would normally never sing without being accompanied by a top level pianist. But in that atmosphere, she just stood up and sang without any accompaniment, in that incredibly beautiful voice of hers, an old spiritual, 'Were You There?'. She then simply and naturally told of her life and the change that had come to it. It cut through the cynicism like a searchlight on a dark night. At the end the editor apologised to Muriel for the way in which he had introduced the evening.

We reached our target of speaking to at least a million people a week through the cinema, the TV and the press.

Our work was a combination of reaching the country as a whole, meeting the leadership, and also working alongside the dockers and *favela* dwellers. We would go to these *favelas*, slum dwellings built on the hills outside Rio where three million people lived, and at the invitation of the *favela* leaders set up a massive screen on some level ground to project the film *Men of Brazil*. The Rio dockers had made this film to tell the story of the change of heart that had come to them as a result of MRA. The hillside was like a giant stadium, with people sitting in front of their shacks as if they were in the gallery of a theatre watching the film below and afterwards hearing the dockers tell of the change that had come to them. It is encouraging that some of the leaders went on to transform the atmosphere in their *favelas,* and still play a big role 30 years on.

One of the leaders we met was the Governor of the most important state. He had been elected on the slogan, 'I may steal, but I do get things done!' We showed *The Crowning Experience* in the Governor's palace for himself and his associates. He was very shaken by it and at the end came up with his wife to talk with Muriel and myself. The first thing Muriel said was, 'How are you going to cure corruption in the state?' I thought his wife would disappear through the floor. He, however, took it seriously, and we had a long talk. The next day he went and made peace with his great enemy, the head of the main newspaper of the state. Again, as in Italy, one doesn't know what long term effects all this has had.

Before I went to South America it was virtually an unknown continent to me. I began to realise what a powerful country Brazil was becoming and was constantly surprised and delighted at the energy and enterprise of its people. Flying half way up the coast from Rio to Recife, I discovered it was the same distance as from London to Istanbul. It wasn't just the size and the richness of resources, but also the contrast between the very rich and the very poor that struck me.

This was particularly focused in the northern area around Recife. The state of Pernambuco, which was largely in the hands of big landowners, was generally dependent on a single crop and became a disaster area if that crop failed. The field workers would then have to travel 2,000 miles to the south in order to find work and survive. They would settle in the *favelas* of Rio or Sao Paulo, often starting another family there, and send back what they could to their wives and children in the north.

I was friendly with an agricultural engineer and asked him one day what quantity of financial aid would be needed to stop these periodical disasters. 'We don't need any aid,' he replied and took me to a map of the state on the wall of his office. He pointed to one area and said, 'In that large estate there is no hunger and no one migrates. The owners have invested their considerable wealth in irrigation and diversification of crops, and the area is prosperous. If the other landowners did the same, and they all could, the state would be transformed.' It emphasised what we already thought, that a change of heart was the key to solving the problems of poverty, hunger and deprivation.

For me personally this was a very important time. Our decision to make these bold moves with the film distribution and TV programmes and with controversial figures like this Governor, were seriously questioned by one of

129

our friends who had previously taken a leading part with MRA in South America. He was in Europe at this time, and I used to quake every time another strongly worded letter arrived telling us how wrong we were. But this helped me to grow out of the habit of conforming to what others thought and to stick by my convictions. This didn't happen in one day, but gradually I began to understand that I must be obedient to the leading of the Holy Spirit, and although I needed to listen to what others said, if I was still certain of that leading, then I must go ahead and obey. It was one of the most important lessons of my life.

The other conclusion I came to, following the South American time, was that if you seriously intend to try and alter things in the world, you have to build a force of people with an experience of transformation in their own lives; at the same time you have to reach masses of people through the media in order to try and alter the whole moral and spiritual climate of a country. The time in Brazil was a practical demonstration of what could be done to reach a whole population if one had access to TV, radio and press.

I rejoined Mary and John in Switzerland when John was going to the little school in Caux. Mary had joined him on her return from South America some months earlier. John had been very well cared for by two friends of ours, Patricia Tremellin and Kristin Squires. But I had been 18 months away from him and Mary nine months. It was only later that I realised that I had got so engrossed in the fascinating campaign in Brazil and that this was too long a time to leave a boy between the ages of four and six. I didn't realise how much a boy needed his father at this point.

Because we felt that we had made this and other mistakes it was an undeserved gift when in the 1980's John came to us, told us things about his own life he had hidden and that he intended to let God run his life from then on.

Since then, after taking two years' training with MRA, he has been in an Insurance Underwriters in the City and established his home in Milton Keynes. He has become a steward at the Methodist Church at Bletchley and takes an active interest in the Westminster Theatre where he is Treasurer of the Friends organisation, and in the MRA Centre at Tirley Garth in Cheshire.

PART III
BRITAIN 1962 – 1994

Chapter 14   MOVING THE MOUNTAIN

THERE was an old man in China who lived by a mountain that blocked his view and so he determined to move it stone by stone. To those who laughed at him he said, 'My sons and their sons will carry stones. The mountain will be moved.'

I once said to a Christian friend who is a well known film actor, 'I sometimes feel as if I am trying to move a mountain with a teaspoon!' He was rather surprised and asked, 'What mountain?' I replied, 'It's the mountain of false values, of gross materialism, secularism and permissiveness which blocks the view of God's wonderful purposes for mankind.'

It's from this mountain that there descends an avalanche of greed, which undermines the efforts to relieve the desperate poverty which continues to mar our world.

It's from this mountain that, through satellite and video, polluted streams flow out to newly liberated countries with false images and distorted values.

I came back to Britain with a growing sense that moving this mountain was my particular calling. This proved to be as great an adventure as the escape from prison camp.

I think I was aware that it is one thing to have a calling and another to equip oneself to fulfil it. Without being fully aware of where it would lead, I was naturally drawn to the Westminster Theatre.

I had given my army gratuity at the end of the war to help buy this theatre, and in 1961 a new phase had started. Until that time it had either been let out to other companies, or used to perform plays by people committed to MRA, of very good standard but mostly by people without professional training.

The one professional taking part in these plays was the well-known actress Phyllis Konstam. She, with her husband Bunny Austin, the tennis star, played a key part in the whole development of theatre by MRA from its beginnings in America.

Largely on the initiative of Peter Howard, Westminster Productions was formed with the aim of presenting plays that would 'not only express the folly of mankind but give people new hope and courage and the will to tackle the problems of the contemporary world.' Fully professional casts and technicians were to be used. There were those who felt that God's truth could only be presented by people who were fully committed to God, but Peter Howard and others felt that British actors and directors, who are amongst the finest in the world and generally of great skill and integrity, could perform his plays.

It was at this time that Kenneth Belden became the Chairman of the Westminster Memorial Trust, who owned the theatre. Due to his vision and dynamic leadership this programme was carried through. Because of his conviction, with the aid of Nigel Morshead, the treasurer, a large sum of money was raised, and the building was doubled in size, making it a very fine complex.

With 15 others I threw myself into making the theatre known. We launched what I believe was the most extensive marketing operation ever undertaken by a single West End theatre. We studied books together on marketing and salesmanship, and we went out and covered every possible source of audiences, social clubs, ticket agencies, schools, tourist agencies, coach companies, churches, and those who organised factory outings. The money to do this came from gifts from our supporters.

As we visited factory social clubs we discovered that there was a great demand for family entertainment, especially at Christmas time. So we wired Peter Howard, who was in America, knowing that he had been thinking of writing a pantomime: 'If you write a pantomime we can sell it.' He wired back immediately, 'I'll write it. It will be called *The Magic Pig*.' As this was already September, when the factory clubs begin to plan their Christmas parties, we wrote to all of them advertising *The Magic Pig*, and bookings started coming in. Then we heard from Peter that he had decided to call it *Give a Dog a Bone*, so we quickly sent out another notice, and that Christmas we were 98 per cent full for the six week run. We then ran it over the Christmas period for 11 seasons.

Another successful area was in education. One of my colleagues, Ken Rundell, created with others a programme for schools called *A Day of London Theatre* which gave school children a glimpse of how a West End production was put together. In an imaginative way they demonstrated on stage how a play was developed from a script through to the opening night, with all the steps involved,

134

*Children at a performance
in the Westminster Theatre*

Photo: Fabian Hodel

including finance, choosing a director, appointing a designer, and casting the actors. Then they would show how
a director works with the cast in rehearsal and give a
glimpse into costume design, lighting, and sound. In the
afternoon the children would see the play we were presenting at that time and follow it with a discussion of the
issues raised in the play. This discussion period was often
the most fruitful time of the day. Joy Weeks, a drama
teacher, continued this work and over the years 200,000
children and staff have attended the 'Day'.

One of my colleagues, David Phillimore, did very effective work in getting tourist agencies to book their organised parties into the theatre – often arranging supper
parties before the show. He made friends with their
London offices as well as visiting them in the United
States, which resulted in a steady flow of tourists.

As regards drawing in the general public, we were less
successful. The task wasn't helped by the fact that the crit-
ics generally ignored what we were doing, viewing it as all
Christian propaganda. So it was difficult to keep the theatre going, and the fact that the period during which we
produced our own plays lasted eight years owes a great
deal to the determination of Kenneth Belden, and to Louis
Fleming and his skill in getting productions together.
Stanley Kiaer, as secretary of the company, played a vital
part in undergirding the whole operation and Don

135

Loughman, the manager for 25 years, was a constant welcoming presence.

There were many others, including the team who worked with me on the marketing, as well as the tireless work of our MRA supporters near London and around the country.

Faithfully our friends in different parts of London, month by month – and sometimes week by week – would bring parties, often coach parties, to see the play that was running. Also at the weekends coach loads would converge on the Westminster from South Wales, the Midlands, the South Coast, Lancashire and Yorkshire and from as far away as Northumberland and Scotland. The effect of the plays on these delegations, very often coming from industrial towns, was far-reaching.

I still hear stories of how people's lives and also of how whole situations were affected by these visits.

Chapter 15   THE NEXT STAGE

ONE day Alan Thornhill, one of whose plays we were presenting at the time, said to me, 'Do you think that if the artistic and dramatic quality of our productions was ten per cent higher, it would affect the size of the audiences?' I had to admit that it would. Although the issues dealt with in our productions were very relevant to the country, and clearly presented an alternative to the philosophy of permissiveness and nihilism which was too often the popular diet of the time, they weren't always of sufficient theatrical and artistic standard to match their rivals. I knew that presenting goodness on the stage was much more difficult than presenting evil and that presenting the truth you believe in might not always be popular. However difficult this might be, I felt that this should be our aim, to present these truths with the very highest theatrical and artistic standards to match what was being done at the National Theatre with the Royal Shakespeare Company, and at other theatres.

By 1969 we were no longer able to go on presenting our own productions. Peter Howard, one of the principal playwrights over that period, had died, and it was getting difficult to find the plays, to fill the seats, and find the finances. So once again the policy became to let the theatre for suitable productions. It was obvious that, if we were to succeed in affecting the values and thinking of the country, then we had to find new writers and wider support.

I even tried my hand at a play myself. It was based on some of the characters I knew in prison camp, an allegory on the question of freedom. I entered it for a competition, and very much to my surprise it won a prize. Henry Cass, the well known director, read it and suggested a play-reading of it with a professional cast. Although well received, I didn't really think that it had a future, nor did I see my role as a playwright. However, I think that it helped me to understand something of the art and the difficulties of writing for theatre, which is so different from other writing.

This was 1970 and we had stopped running our own

plays at the theatre, when two friends of mine, Ailsa Hamilton and Juliet Boobbyer, asked me if I would collaborate with them in creating and producing a multi-media show on the life of Frank Buchman, the initiator of Moral Re-Armament. This show used film clips, animation, stills, cartoons and even some of my watercolour paintings of the Lake District. It also had a small, live musical group. We called it *Cross Road*. We had two runs at the Westminster Theatre; then we made it into a travelling show, took it round the country, and eventually produced it as a film. The professional excellence of the film-maker, David Channer, and Peter Sisam and the designing skill of Bill Cameron-Johnson made this possible. I think it helped people to understand the nature and purpose of Frank Buchman's work, his insistence on a personal change of heart, rooted in his own experience of what the Cross meant.

Buchman had for some years been responsible for a successful social work programme for deprived children in Philadelphia. As has happened so often to those engaged in this kind of work, the committee responsible had refused to allocate the funding needed, so he had resigned. He had become filled with bitterness at the destruction of what he felt was his life's work.

Visiting Keswick in the English Lake District, in a little Methodist chapel he heard a woman speak of the Cross of Christ. It was a turning point in his life. It came home to him that his bitterness against the committee meant that he was crucifying Christ. He wrote letters of apology, and this was the beginning of the new life and power.

Collaborating with this production gave me a further insight into what went into the writing and production of a West End play and also of a touring show. This was a significant step in learning.

This point in my work with theatre was similar to one stage I reached during my escape: would I ever get to the fighting line and get through it to freedom? Now the question was, would we ever be able to reach the standards needed and reach out to the whole country through the media?

With Westminster Productions we had made a sortie, and certainly in the field of children's entertainment had made an impact, but it was just a beginning.

If we had the serious intent to help 'Thy Kingdom come', it was obviously necessary to affect the values and life-styles of people through the most potent means

138

available, certainly the theatre, which so often sets the trend for TV, but also the whole of the media. I felt that if we didn't tackle this high ground, it meant that we weren't in earnest. A seemingly impossible job, but one to be aimed at.

The task of trying to portray Christian truth and values is a testing one. Obviously, to be effective, what one wants to convey must not be something merely placed in the mouth of one of the characters in a play; it has to be integral to the story itself. It must be an experience for the audience as they live through the action on stage or in a film.

One play I saw at that time was Arthur Miller's *The Crucible* performed at the National. I went with a certain pre-judgement about it, having heard that it had a political motivation. But I found myself deeply involved with the character of John Proctor, wonderfully played by Colin Blakely. I lived through his dilemma as he faced the choice of admitting his affair with a young woman, and thereby losing his whole reputation in that close-knit community, while knowing that by hiding the truth he would be furthering the great wrongs that were being done. To me it conveyed a very moving message on the importance of honesty and integrity.

Many people say that there is something wrong in trying to convey a message through a play or film, and that it isn't art to do so. The fact is that in any play worth anything, there is some message involved. It may simply be that there is nothing in life worth stating, worth giving a message about, or that money, or sex, or power is the thing that really matters; or as with many of Shakespeare's plays, it may be cautionary, showing the inevitable result of unlimited ambition, jealousy or greed.

The glib presentation when everything works out well in the end is generally not very convincing, for so few people share that experience. The story of a man or a woman who chooses a certain course of action, and the struggle they go through, is both exciting and believable. There are so many stories past and present of this kind of struggle, and they do make good theatre.

Chapter 16   INTEGRITY

I REALISED that to be equipped for the calling also involved an inner transformation and the importance of integrity and wholeness. At most stages of my life I had had two faces. In school days there was the one at school and quite a different one at home and at church. When I joined the army I made a deliberate attempt to assume the speech and attitude of an officer. I have often said jokingly that I got my commission through growing the right kind of moustache. However, when I was posted to the Northumberland Hussars it was more difficult. Our adjutant was the Duke of Northumberland and nearly all of the officers were landowners. It was clearly impossible for me to pretend to be of the hunting, shooting and fishing fraternity, and I began to realise that people were more likely to respect me if I was fully identified with my own background rather than trying to put on an act.

Later on, when I was living at the MRA centre in London and going out each day to my job in Army Education, I remember having consciously to switch my attitude as I returned to where I was living. It wasn't so much that I compromised my principles but that there was a different group of people to please. In the following years I looked up to, admired and tried to copy many of those who were giving leadership in MRA. Forty of us, went over to the USA at this time, and I recall being suddenly struck by the fact that these were not super men and women to be idolised or looked up to, but people who needed thought and care just like everyone else.

In those post-war years the work of MRA depended a great deal on the wonderful leadership given by Frank Buchman and Peter Howard. I know now that we often failed them by not giving them the vigorous and questioning fellowship that everyone needs. One result of this was a tendency to go overboard on any particular issue they stressed. For instance the Communist influence in the trades unions and many areas of life was a very real danger, but in our enthusiasm we began to see 'a red under every bed'. More importantly it meant we paid less attention to the secularisation of our own society and the rapid erosion of values. I remember a leading journalist who knew the work well saying that he always knew what the views would be of anyone in MRA, implying that we all followed a 'party line'.

This was happening at a time when the work of MRA was exerting a very powerful influence. The conferences at Caux in Switzerland and at Mackinac in the USA were not only overflowing but were drawing leading figures such as Robert Schuman, the Foreign Minister of France, and Konrad Adenauer, the German Chancellor. Both France and Germany gave honours to Frank Buchman for the part that MRA was playing in bringing their two nations together. In the continent of Africa, where many countries were moving towards their independence, leaders responded to MRA because of the vision it gave for their nationhood. MRA was also encouraging a profound reconciliation between former enemies in Asia.

I suppose that it is true that success is more dangerous to the work of the Spirit than failure.

Even after Buchman and Howard died I found that I often asked myself, 'What would either of them have done in this circumstance?' This was a real block to the working of the Holy Spirit, and we could have avoided many mistakes if each of us had been free channels of the Holy Spirit instead of conforming to what we thought others would expect of us. It wasn't, of course, always easy to go against the trend or to question those who were giving leadership at the time. Several times when I did that I encountered intense disapproval. There was also a danger of manoeuvring to get one's own particular conviction advanced.

As more and more of us associated with MRA have grown out of this conformism, so the work has largely shaken off these tendencies and become a much freer instrument of the Holy Spirit. I think that with every movement of the Spirit down the ages, this combination of individual calling and dependence on the Spirit, with being part of a fellowship, has been difficult to achieve. To maintain the delicate balance of the freedom of moving with the Holy Spirit while remaining of one heart and mind with a group of close friends is never easy.

We are rather like ships, starting in a harbour, but having at a certain point to break free of the safe haven and venture out as a free-booter over the seven seas. At the same time we have to keep an intense loyalty to the Commander-in-Chief and be ready at any moment to take

142

part in a combined operation. Those who do this live life fully, taking risks and of course making mistakes, but enjoy the excitement and fullness of a life committed to big tasks.

The integrity of our lives, with our every relationship based on our relationship with the Creator, is, I believe, all important.

Chapter 17   BECOMING AN IMPRESARIO

BECOMING an impresario was a major step. I had learnt in
the 1950s and 1960s that the ways of the Holy Spirit are
unexpected and generally started with obedience to a
simple thought. In 1973 I saw an amateur production of a
new musical about John Wesley called *Ride! Ride!* by Alan
Thornhill with music by Penelope Thwaites. Alan had
been encouraged to write this musical by two of our most
prominent Methodist figures – Maldwyn Edwards and
Benson Perkins. Shortly afterwards I was having my usual
time of quiet in the morning, when the thought came into
my mind, 'The Methodist Church will take this musical to
the whole country.' I didn't take it too seriously, but I
happened to mention the thought to some of my
colleagues. One of them said, 'Well, if you think it might
come from the good Lord, hadn't you better do something
about it?'

So I wrote to Leslie Marsh, the Secretary of the Methodist Drama Committee who had been responsible for the
amateur production, and he and Dr John Gibbs, the Chairman of the committee and a leading figure in the church
who shared my vision of Christian theatre, came to lunch
and talked over the possibilities. This led to another production put on by John and Sheila Gibbs in South Wales
and taken to that year's Methodist Conference.

A year later we met at the Methodist Central Hall with
many of the leaders of Methodism to discuss the idea of a
professional production. There was an interesting division
of opinion. Some said if we could find the money we
should go ahead and do a professional production. Others
said it is what God wants; we should go ahead, and the
money will come. John Gibbs then made it very practical
by committing his family trust to give £10,000; I promised I
would raise another £10,000.

I had no idea how I would do this, but Mary and I
started by visiting the district chairmen of the Methodist
Church in the major centres of the country. Everywhere
they said, 'Yes, it should be done, but not just in London;
bring it here to Birmingham, Manchester, Liverpool,

145

Dr and Mrs John Gibbs

Nottingham, Newcastle, etc.' My reply was, 'Will you introduce me to at least two people who will give £1,000 each? At this point we are only interested in big donations. Smaller ones can come later.' In each district I was given introductions, and to my delight £2,000 came immediately from one lady in the first place we visited and £1,000 from others. When the Methodist Conference convened again in June, we had £30,000.

Later that year we formed a charitable company and called it Aldersgate Productions. John Gibbs suggested this name; many people would know that it was at Aldersgate Street in the City of London that John Wesley had the heart-warming experience which changed his life; others, he argued, would think it sounded like a good sound city name.

We appointed one of the best known directors of musicals, the late Peter Coe, and started to find the cast and technical staff. At this point I remember walking around the roads near my home one evening and realising that we had committed ourselves to an expense of £120,000, and we had promises of only £30,000. (It would be at least five times that amount today.) If the Methodist people didn't rally round to fill the theatres, we would really be sunk. In a Don Camillo-like discussion with the Almighty I remember asking, 'What have you got me into?', and the reply came, 'I told you to do it. Have no fear.' Tony Bigland, a close friend and colleague, and I went round the country

146

and booked the theatres. We again saw the Methodist district chairmen and asked them to appoint one of their most active and competent people to get to work and fill the theatres we had booked. They were all large theatres, with capacities of between 10,000 and 20,000 for the week's run. Some of these men proved to be exceptionally brilliant; in some cases the theatres were filled by parties for the entire week before the run started.

Although I had had by now a dozen years of experience in theatre, especially in marketing, it was a bold step, and some considered it a foolish one, to take on a national tour of a big musical with a top director. But it was a very necessary step in fulfilling my calling. The skills to be learnt were many: budgeting; negotiating percentages and ticket prices with theatre managers; choosing a director and fixing his fees and percentages; finding a musical director, set and costume designers, a lighting and sound designer; and then appointing a company manager and stage manager, who are so important in creating the right spirit in the cast. Finally auditioning the cast and choosing the musicians with all the union rules involved – and arranging the tour itself. I had to learn all this quickly but was greatly helped by Bill Cameron-Johnson, who designed a really wonderful set for the show, and by my friend Hugh Williams who took on the task of production manager.

Hugh, who from the 1960s has also shared fully this commitment to 'move the mountain', had started to work with MRA after leaving Oxford. His first task had been as ASM (Assistant Stage Manager) for some of the plays – ASM is the lowest form of life in the theatre, making cups of tea and doing the odd jobs – quite a step down for an Oxford graduate. Since then he has tackled every aspect of theatre – as stage manager, company manager, production manager, actor, director, producer and especially writing for theatre.

His friendship, and that of his wife Dell, has been a constant strength over the years. We have shared most experiences – including both developing heart trouble and having operations at the same time and having been through various ups and downs together. Our most recent crisis was when in 1993 Dell's cancer was diagnosed. Fortunately after a successful operation and chemo-therapy, it has been cleared up.

Without Hugh I couldn't possibly have coped with *Ride! Ride!*. Also it was a help to have Nancy Ruthven and Chris Channer, both accomplished actresses, in the cast and both

147

Hugh and Dell Williams

committed Christians.

The most testing area was in working with a high powered director who always wanted his own way, as most directors do. A crucial point in our relationship came after the opening week at Nottingham Theatre Royal. Alan Thornhill, the author, John Gibbs, the Chairman of Aldersgate, and I felt that certain things had crept into the show during rehearsal which detracted from it rather than enhanced it. So I went down to see Peter Coe at his home in Surrey and explained that the three of us had agreed on four points that needed to be altered.Even though they weren't very big points, Peter argued strongly against them being changed, but eventually said, 'Well you are the producer, so I'll have to do as you say.' At Bradford the show was to be given a final polish, having had two weeks to 'run in'. It incidentally played to full houses.

I well remember Peter coming up to me and saying in his courteous manner – he was a very courteous man – 'Ronald, you know I don't agree with the points you want altered, so I think it would be best if you would talk to the cast yourself about them.' So I innocently walked on to the stage where they were going to start rehearsals and started to outline the changes. Immediately I sensed a wave of hostility. Peter had obviously talked to them about it already and persuaded them that our points were mistaken. A director has great influence on actors: after all, their getting further work is so often dependent on their relationship with him.

Can you imagine the scene with 22 angry well-established actors surrounding this beginner? I quickly said a silent prayer whilst the protests were flying around

148

'Ride! Ride!' – Peter Coe (above) directing
starring Gordon Gostelow, Caroline Villiers, Brendon Barry

and then said to them, 'You are all experienced professional actors, and you know that your task is to interpret
for an audience the ideas and purpose of the author and
producer. I trust your integrity in this, and so I'm not

149

going to tell you how to make the alterations or to give you a deadline for them but trust that you will work out the best way of doing them, and I leave it up to you.' The very next day all but one had been altered, and the last one was eventually corrected.

One of the most memorable moments of theatre was at Newcastle. Peter Coe had suggested to Alan Thornhill that the play should open with some words of John Wesley which Gordon Gostelow, who played the part, should speak directly to the audience. Alan and I were a bit doubtful about beginning in this way, as it seemed so like giving a sermon, but it worked well. At Newcastle that year there had been the scandal of Dan Smith, who had cheated the local authority of a great deal of money and been convicted of corruption by the courts. Gordon came forward with the opening words, 'Let me ask you in tender love. Is this city of Newcastle a Christian city? Are you living portraits of Jesus Christ whom you leaders are appointed to represent among men? Are you not a generation of triflers, triflers with your God, triflers with one another?' When he came to the sentence, 'And are your magistrates honest and all your heads of government all of one heart and soul?', a loud voice came from the upper circle, 'By golly, they are not,' which brought a great wave of laughter and applause from the audience and was a wonderful start to the evening.

It was one thing to have had the idea that the Methodist Church should take *Ride! Ride!* to the country. It was quite another experience to stand in the foyers of the theatres and see the crowds pour in night after night. And also to be there at the end when my friends Tony and Yvonne Bigland sold the beautiful souvenir brochure, designed by Dell Williams and Ailsa Hamilton, to the crowds coming out, so that they could take home something of the story and words of John Wesley. It was very encouraging to see the fruits of obedience. Perhaps a stone had been moved in the mountain?

When we were preparing *Ride! Ride!*, I read the whole of John Wesley's journals and many of the multitude of books written about him. Like many Methodists I knew about his heart-warming experience in Aldersgate Street but had little idea of the man himself. He had ridden 250,000 miles on horseback. He would preach at 5 o'clock most mornings and spent five hours in reading and meditation each day,

Opposite: Plate 5 — 'The Langdale Pikes'

The Duke and Duchess of Gloucester at the Royal Premiere of 'Ride! Ride!'

often whilst on horseback. I was struck by his insistence that the newly converted should stick together, often quoting the words, 'Unless you bind people together you are making a rope of sand.' Wesley's other passion was that his followers should study the Bible and other books, and then rigorously apply their new-found faith to their communities and in their work place. Reading Bready's book *England Before and After Wesley* I came to understand the great social transformation that he engendered, and the fact that the abolition of the slave trade, the enactment of the factory laws, and the formation of trades unions, all owed a great deal to this one man's work and passion.

We toured 11 cities on what is known as the No 1 Circuit, at the most prestigious theatres, and then played 11 weeks at the Westminster, starting with a gala performance attended by the Duke and Duchess of Gloucester. Some of the press applauded the play; others didn't, but the *Guardian* called it, 'One of the most astonishing theatrical events we are likely to see this year.' Over 100,000 people saw it. What delighted us most were the stories of people's lives being affected by it, such as the minister who wrote to the *Methodist Recorder* saying that his whole ministry had been renewed.

Opposite: Plate 6 – 'Clothed in Light'

I remember one amusing incident. I was invited to address the London NE Synod at Chelmsford. As I travelled down in the train I was joined in the seat opposite by a minister; we started talking and I found out that he was going to this Synod. After I had told him that I had been invited to speak about *Ride! Ride!* and that after the tour it was coming in to the Westminster, he started to tell me with some force all that he didn't like about those 'Moral Re-Armament people' who owned the Westminster. Later he turned to me and said, 'What do you do, Mr Mann, besides producing plays?' 'Oh, I said, I work with Moral Re-Armament,' at which point we both roared with laughter and from then on became great friends.

After seeing the musical, Benson Perkins, an elder statesman of Methodism, aged nearly 90, said how wonderful it was but added, 'I'm not sure some of my older colleagues will like it.'

Since 1976 *Ride! Ride!* has been performed extensively in the United States of America and many other parts of the world, and at the World Methodist Conference in Dublin. As I write this, it has just been produced in Guatemala, the Midwest of America, and by an amateur company in Kent.

In 1987 the director Norman Stone and writer/actor John Wells asked us (Aldersgate) to collaborate with them in producing a TV series about John Wesley. We were able to find some initial finance for this and to interest Bob Feaster, head of the United Methodist Publishing House in the United States, in the project. An excellent script entitled *The Burning* was prepared and negotiations were started with the BBC. Twice it looked as though we would have a co-production but this fell through at the last minute both times.

John Wells, having great conviction about this, persisted and working with Bob Feaster arranged a workshop production with the Royal Shakespeare Company (RSC). In November 1994 it was rehearsed at Stratford and then performed in public in January 1995. Some of the Aldersgate Board and the entire Board of the United Methodist Publishing House came over from the United States for a special performance on January 10th.

It proved to be a superb production, authentic in every detail and very moving.

The Board of the publishing house met afterwards and it was agreed with John Wells and the RSC that they would tour it around some of the major cities in the United States, and eventually make a film or video.

People still talk to me about *Ride! Ride!* and the effect it had on them. Many leaders of the other churches came to see it, and when we asked them, 'Is this what the Church should be doing?', they agreed heartily. So our board became ecumenical, with Anglicans, Roman Catholics, United Reformed Church, and Baptists added to it.

It was only later that I realised where the Holy Spirit was leading us. It had happened so naturally. All the different denominations had become our partners. There was no longer a question of one group doing it alone.The whole Church, was being drawn into this task. We stated our aim simply: 'To provide first class professional theatre which conveys Christian truth in such a way that it can entertain, enlighten, educate, and open the door to faith.' However it seems to take time for churchmen to understand the importance of what we are trying to do. I recall one leading churchman who came to see *Ride! Ride!*. He was delighted with it and we talked quite often with him about our aim. A year later when he came to see Hugh Williams's play *Fire*, he turned to me at the end and said, 'You know, Mr Mann, this is a way of getting the Christian Gospel across!'

From 1976 until 1990 we were in almost continuous production with a great variety of shows, ranging from plays about the lives of St Francis and St Paul to modern dramas dealing with current issues such as euthanasia. There were also many children's plays.

During these years I often got what my wife Mary calls 'productionitis', waking up very early in the morning wondering how we were going to get through this or that crisis. Constant risk-taking and being always in need of a miracle, financial or otherwise, I discovered, helped one's faith to grow. If you are out on a limb, having to pray your way through difficulties but still surviving, it brings a reliance on the direction of the Holy Spirit just as the dangers and uncertainties I had encountered during my escape had done. Perhaps the most telling examples of this have been to do with finance. In present values we have had to find almost a million pounds for this work, but it has always come, often at the last moment.

* * * * *

For 12 years I was a member of the prestigious Society of West End Managers, and I had to learn what is involved in being a theatrical producer, an impresario.

153

The first task is choosing a play. This may be through a script that is presented to you for consideration, or it may be a play that you commission. Writers approach playwriting in different ways. Some, like Peter Howard, write plays because they feel something urgently needs to be said. So Howard wrote on themes such as what would happen in a newspaper office if a young reporter tried to be honest. Other plays have been based on historical figures, such as Robert Bolt's *A Man For All Seasons* about Sir Thomas More. Another approach is to see certain characters in a given situation and, having envisaged them, to let them develop without even knowing what will eventually happen. Thus C S Lewis suddenly had a picture in his mind one day of a 'Faun with an umbrella walking through a snow covered path in the middle of a wood, and coming across a lamppost.' From this picture he developed the story of *The Lion, the Witch and the Wardrobe*, and subsequently the whole Narnia series.

From our point of view there are several important criteria. Does the play throw any light on the 'human condition' and portray something of truth about life? Will it enlighten people, help them understand life and perhaps help them live it more fully? Could it have some part in 'opening the door to faith'? Equal with these – is the play well written, and will it stand up to the tough West End scene? Is it artistically and dramatically successful? Is it entertaining, and will it hold an audience? Not even the most experienced producers have always been able to decide this, a fact to which the great number of flops among new plays bears witness. Until a play is actually seen on stage, it is very difficult to judge.

This is why producers will try out a new play round the country or at a local repertory theatre before bringing it to London, and even then there is no guarantee of its success, as London is very different to other places. Alan Ayckbourn, one of today's most successful playwrights, tries his plays out at the theatre he runs at Scarborough. A successful play is a combination of the skill of the playwright and of the director, as well as the actors, and the final result is always a question of getting all of this right.

One of the plays that I had great hopes for was *Man of Two Worlds* about St Paul. I made the mistake of trying to get it on quickly, when I should have waited to get the director I wanted for it. My colleague, Hugh Williams, questioned the timing, but I felt at that stage it was too late to stop. The play helped some people. The director's sister told us that she returned to her Catholic faith because of it. I became aware through this, and other mistakes I made, of certain things in my own nature. As a schoolboy I was a long-distance runner and generally won. At rugby I was always able to keep moving right to the end, and in the army I won the mountain races. So I was always loath to give up on anything I started. This can be a valuable quality, but often it has meant that I haven't stopped long enough to ask God, 'I know this started with what I believed was an inspired thought, but do I still go on, or is there a new direction? It has led to major mistakes, which when you are presenting plays, affect a lot of people. I have come to feel what our grandparents called a conviction of sin – and I hope I've learnt the lesson. I've been much helped in this by my wife, Mary, who gently points out that 'the drive is on'. Fortunately God forgives and often uses our mistakes.

As well as the script of the play, the next most important factor is the director. His task is to transfer the written word into a live spectacle on a stage. His integrity and faithfulness is of prime importance. He has to visualise how the play will look up there on a stage: the action, the sets, costumes and lighting. It depends largely on him and his collaboration with the designers whether his vision will be fulfilled.

Finally his choice of actors, generally made with the producer, is vital. Wrong casting has ruined more plays than probably anything else. I've known us to go through a list of as many as 30 names, talking to them or their agents before being able to cast a leading part. Having chosen the cast, the director has to draw the depth from inside the actor so that the character becomes three dimensional.

One example of this was with the play *Fire*, by Hugh Williams, a modern drama about a director who tries to live out his newly-found Christian faith in the difficult world of the professional theatre. In order to have a well-known name – someone who had a reputation in films – we miscast one of the four parts and so weakened what could have been a very powerful play.

Different directors have different approaches and skills. Some, especially those who specialise in musicals, depend a great deal on the visual, others on the words. Some are skilled in bringing new meaning to a classic, others are at their best delving into the meaning of a completely new play. The director's personal beliefs may not always be

155

important. One of the finest directors we saw at work directing a strong play with a Christian message was a man who called himself a lapsed Jew.

Of course it is unwise to appoint someone who is deeply and fundamentally opposed to your aims, but above all a director needs real integrity in his work of putting on stage what the playwright wants.

Finance plays a very crucial part in producing. You can't put on a play without financial backing. This can be by subsidy from the Arts Council or a local authority, or it can be from trusts and individuals who want to support what you are doing. Most commercial productions are financed by 'angels' – people who back plays as a risk investment. I have never managed to get a grant from the Arts Council, although I have applied a number of times. The last time I saw them, I said, 'Tell me why it is that you never give us a grant.' The two people I was talking to smiled and said, 'I suppose it's because you are so good at raising money.' I replied with some force, 'You mean to say that anyone who is business-like and doesn't go into debt, you don't support, and those who don't handle their affairs as well, you do support?' They smiled again and said, 'Well, it looks like that.' However, I think part of it was that they somehow felt that as we were a Christian body, we weren't quite 'theatre' – an idea which they denied and which we've tried hard to alter.

Most of our support has come from trusts and individuals. As I mentioned with *Ride! Ride!*, Dr Gibbs and his family trust were key to the whole move, and they have continued to support Aldersgate in a marvellous way. I felt that John Gibbs and his family regarded themselves as stewards for the resources they had, and during our 18 years of working together I never needed to suggest when they should help. John, as Chairman of Aldersgate, knew the needs, and I knew that they would do with their resources what they felt the good Lord wanted them to.

With investors we had to make sure that they knew it was a risk investment. Some, with *Ride! Ride!* didn't seem to be aware of this, so when I found that we couldn't pay them back in full, I asked some of them whether they would like to consider their investment as a gift for the work of the company. Some were very pleased to do this; others didn't want to, so we paid what we could then, and over the next two years I held exhibitions of my paintings and from the proceeds was able to pay them all in full.

Over these 18 years I realise that at any given moment

156

we have always been in need of £10,000, often much more, with no knowledge of where it was to come from, but the certainty that if we didn't find it we would be faced with insolvency. This is where prayer comes in, along with making our needs known. There was also the need for long-term work with trusts. One large trust, whom we thought would back us initially, didn't do so, saying that their purpose was evangelism, indicating that they didn't see this as having anything to do with this purpose. The secretary of the trust viewed the matter positively, so he began to bring in some of the trustees to lunch with us so that they could understand that the kind of theatre we were doing could be considered as pre-evangelism – turning over the ground so that the seed could be sown. They became one of our greatest supporters. We invited members of trusts to see our productions so that they could evaluate our worth for themselves. We had to learn to care for them as people, and not just as a source of income, and I'm glad to say that many have become personal friends.

The most difficult and important part of producing is marketing and publicity. It has been said that half the money spent on publicity is wasted, but no one knows which half.

I remember a phone conversation with the producer, Cameron Mackintosh, after the tour of *Ride! Ride!*. At the time he was struggling to find his way, but he has since become the most successful producer in the business, with musicals running in most of the capitals of the world. (At the moment he has five musicals in London, including *Les Miserables* in the West End, and has just endowed a chair for theatre studies in Oxford.) 'How on earth did you fill those theatres?' he asked, and then answered his own question, 'Of course, you have your mafia!' From that time on we called our Aldersgate mailing list the 'Mafia file'.

The great fascination of producing is to watch the development of a single idea through commissioning an author to write the play, then through all the stages until you are there on the first night, watching the audience pour into the theatre.

Of course not every play succeeds as you hoped it would, and I don't know how often we managed to raise the artistic and dramatic standard of the play in the way that Alan Thornhill had hoped.

It is said in theatre circles that a producer will run out of steam and creative ideas after about eight years. Producing is one of the most hazardous, exhausting, and exhilarating tasks that anyone can take on. I've often replied, when people have asked me if everything isn't an anti-climax after my wartime experience, 'Oh no, the last ten years have been just as exciting and, in a different way, just as perilous.'

Becoming an impresario was an exciting but very demanding business, but I was greatly helped by having a series of excellent PA's starting with Vilma Maritz from South Africa, and then Judy Newell. Buzz Low, Jean Wheeliker, Adele Franklin (who then married our company manager, Howard Bird) and finally Teresa Dadey. I think it probably true to say that by relieving the pressure they kept me alive.

Chapter 18   FINDING ALLIES

I THINK it's a common experience, when one starts on a calling, to feel somewhat alone. Then suddenly you find allies in the task – people with a similar or even greater commitment. This happened continuously to me through those years. One of the first allies was Nigel Goodwin*. Nigel is an unforgettable character not just for his colourful dress, favouring greens and purples, but above all for the way he pours himself out to everyone he meets, whether it be ordinary folk or international stars of stage and screen. Many of these have become close personal friends who rely greatly on him for help and inspiration.

He started life as an actor, brought up in a divided home without any background of faith. In his twenties he had his own 'heart-warming experience of Christ'. He then took two years out of the theatre world at a Bible college. Then he felt a strong calling to care for actors and artists of other disciplines working in their professional fields.

Along with Cliff Richard and David Winter, who later became head of religious broadcasting for the BBC, Nigel formed the Arts Centre Group in London, and subsequently other groups round the country, so that Christians in the midst of the stress of their professional lives would have support and become as he often says, thoroughly Christian, thoroughly professional. Since then he has extended this work all round the world and formed Genesis Arts Trust to make it possible. We invited Nigel to join our Aldersgate Board, and with his inside knowledge of the theatre world and of a great many actors, this was invaluable.

Perhaps his main contribution was a deeper one. I discovered that in any gathering he seemed to sense where there was a need and sought to find a way to meet it. It might be someone who was discouraged or in difficulties,

---

*The biography of Nigel Goodwin, *Arts and Minds*, was published by Hodder and Stoughton in 1994.

Nigel and Gillian Goodwin

Photo: Hanne Jordan

or who needed correction. My tendency was to want to get on with the business in hand, but gradually I learnt from Nigel that people were much more important than plans, and that the best plans would come out of the growth in people.

Another important ally was Daniel Pearce. He wrote to us at the Westminster Theatre sending us a play which he had written. Although it wasn't a play we wanted to produce it was very well written, so we asked him in to lunch and learnt of his life. He was an American who had come over to England with a sense of calling to join the Anglican order, The Community of the Resurrection. Eventually he'd been accepted as a monk of that order and had gone out to Rhodesia, as it was then, to teach in their school there.

Having always been keen on theatre, he wrote plays for his students and eventually was awarded a national prize for his playwriting. He then became headmaster of the college and whilst in that position had a crucial experience which he told us about. He was having great trouble, both with the staff and with a group of students, one of whom he had always found particularly trying. He was wondering whether he ought to expel the young man, but questioned whether this was justified or only giving vent to his prejudices against someone with a reputation as a trouble-maker. After a very unsatisfactory interview with this 18-year-old which only confirmed his reputation, the boy turned to him from the doorway and said, 'Sir, I think you need to be filled with the Holy Spirit.' Daniel's reaction was anger. He felt like shouting at him, 'I am the Head of the school, your Headmaster, and what right have you to

160

say this?' Instead of this he found himself saying, 'Yes, I do!' The boy looked astounded. He later told Daniel that he had had no intention of saying these words, but that they had suddenly come to him.

Daniel, being a man of integrity, prayed to be filled with the Holy Spirit, which began a change in his life not only affecting this boy but also the staff and his whole future. He told us that for the first time he really understood the love of God.

We became close friends. We sensed that here was a man of God who also had a great gift as a playwright, and who had been led to us.

It was shortly after this meeting, when searching for a subject for a play, that I remembered having read many years before C S Lewis's book *Surprised by Joy*, the fascinating story of a man who had become a Christian largely through his intellect. It wasn't until his wife, whom he married late in life, died of cancer, that after a period of deep distress and doubt, his faith became also a matter of the heart and emotion. Could it work as a play?

I talked with David William, who had directed a play for us, and asked him what he thought of the idea. He responded enthusiastically; he had studied under C S Lewis at Oxford and added, 'If I were you, I would ask Daniel Pearce to write it.' He had already read some of Daniel's work.

So *Song of the Lion*, as it was called, was born. Perhaps more than any other play, I felt it achieved what we had set out to do. It was a production which seemed to reach

Daniel Pearce

David William directing
Hugh Manning in
'Song of the Lion'

into people's hearts. Perhaps the most penetrating scene is towards the end, when Lewis is in complete despair after the death of his wife Joy. He no longer even remembers her face and he wonders whether God is not after all a 'cosmic sadist'. He says, 'Then after ten days of low-hung grey skies and motionless warm dampness, the sun was shining and there was a light breeze and suddenly at the very moment when so far I mourned Joy least, I remembered her best. Indeed it was something almost better than memory. It was as if the lifting of the sorrow removed a barrier. God always knew that my temple was a house of cards. His only way of making me realise the fact was to knock it down. To admit God exists, as I did in that Oxford study in 1929, is only the beginning.'

The ending was especially effective, and this came out of some conflict. Daniel, with the encouragement of David William, had written a brilliant but very intellectual final passage. John Gibbs and I felt that it was way above most people's heads, but we agreed that it should be tried out during the previews. One of David William's friends, a personality in the theatre world, said to him after the performance, 'Wonderful, but you need a new ending!' So we put our heads together, and Hugh Manning, who was playing the part of Lewis, suggested that the words from Lewis's book, *The Last Battle*, might be the right ones. In this final scene Lewis takes all his many books, which represent his life's work, and puts them in a great pile on the floor. He then quietly turns from them and looks towards the door which opens and from which comes a very bright light. As he turns and walks towards the door, he says

162

'The term is over... The holidays have begun... The dream is ended... This is the morning...'

I know people for whom this was a very deep experience.

Howard Bird, who had come to us as stage manager for *Song of the Lion* and, during his stay over several years, become a convinced Christian, told us that Vanessa Ford, whom he had worked with, had been trying to get the rights for C S Lewis's *The Lion, the Witch and the Wardrobe* but had failed. Could I help?

The executors and agents of C S Lewis had been enthusiastic about *Song of the Lion*, so a meeting was arranged and because of this good will and the Westminster's reputation for its schools' programme and children's shows, the permission was granted. *The Lion, the Witch and the Wardrobe* was produced by Aldersgate and Westminster Productions, with Vanessa Ford Productions.

This was such a success at the Westminster that Vanessa Ford, who had considerable experience of touring, took it all around the country. This was followed by two other plays based on the Narnia books which reached, in the next five years about a million and a half children and their families.

What pleased me most about it was that when I talked to the children after the performances and asked them who was their favourite character, they would generally say, 'Oh Aslan, good old Aslan'. Aslan is the lion who comes to save Narnia from the evil White Witch. He is a 'Christ figure'. To make goodness attractive on the stage is the most difficult task, and in these plays it succeeded. The play also worked for people on different levels. For many it was just a good adventure story, for others a symbol of the battle between good and evil, while for yet others it was a parallel with the redemption of Christ.

We worked with Vanessa and her husband Glyn (who did the stage adaptation of the book) for five years. It wasn't always easy, but Stanley Kiaer, representing Westminster Productions, and I did enjoy working with this dynamic young woman.

I don't think it's too much to claim that it was largely due to the success of these productions that the TV film of *Shadowlands* was created. The head of religious broadcasting for the BBC described *Shadowlands* as having done more to present Christianity to the British public than anything else.

Shadowlands on TV was followed by the play, which ran

for over a year and finally by the Richard Attenborough film – which incidentally has provoked the usual wave of debunking one has come to expect. One critic accused Lewis of harbouring a sado-masochistic sexuality, being an alcoholic and much else. To those who knew Lewis and his writings it seemed that the play seriously undervalued the enormous impact of Lewis's writings, broadcasts, and his books (which are published now in millions of copies), and also underplayed Lewis's final conversion, which was the strong point in Daniel Pearce's play. However, almost everyone I have talked to has been deeply moved by Attenborough's film.

This, I think, was one more stone in the mountain that was moved.

The encounter with Daniel Pearce was a very important step forward in the quality of the plays we were producing, and also in our outreach through the Narnia plays. The whole process of preparing these plays based on C S Lewis was a very rewarding one for me personally, too.

I read all of Lewis's books with the exception of some of those of literary criticism. One in particular had a permanent affect on my life. It was a talk he gave in Oxford called *Weight of Glory*. In this he describes in his most vivid way the kind of glory which is the destiny of human beings. Having made this very real, he then says, 'And what has this got to do with how we are tomorrow morning here in Oxford? If with every person we meet, we realise that they could become so glorious that we might want to bow down before them, or that they might become more terrible than the worst horrors we could imagine, and that our touch with them might decide which of these alternatives they become, then this talk will have been worthwhile.'

Ever since I read that some 15 years ago, I have been reminded of it daily. Meeting with all the people I do, and the people I pass in the street – and even my colleagues whom I've got used to – I think, 'This person is beloved of God' and look at them differently.

I have begun to learn not to have what one of my friends called 'a hidden agenda' – always on the look-out as to how someone I knew or met could further my particular objectives.

It was all part of learning that although I had a particular calling it was still only a part of my overall calling of, as Pope John Paul expresses it, 'renewing the face of the earth'.

164

The Lion , the Witch and the Wardrobe

These lessons were reinforced by an invitation to see a play at the Bridge Park community centre in North London. I was impressed by the play but even more by the extraordinary story of the men running the centre, Leonard Johnson and Lawrence Fearon, who had both served prison sentences and then had a very real Christian experience. They had gone on to help create this £6 million community centre, Bridge Park, to meet the needs of their deprived community. We became close friends. They came to the MRA centres at Tirley Garth and Caux and so Mary and I became involved in friendships with many people who are grappling with the inner city problems.

Another ally on the road was Malcolm Muggeridge. He had collaborated with Alan Thornhill in writing a play about euthanasia called *Sentenced to Life!*, and they approached me about producing it.

We undertook the task and a fascinating friendship began. At that time Malcolm was very much in the public eye, so we were able to get a great deal of media coverage. When we held a reception for the press, people flocked in to hear what it was all about.

165

Alan Thornhill and Malcolm Muggeridge

Malcolm held strong views on most issues. He was in favour of capital punishment, saying in his provocative way, 'If the Romans hadn't had capital punishment, we wouldn't have had the Crucifixion!' He held strong views on abortion. He had strong views about most of the churches and church leaders. He had perhaps the strongest views of all about television. He used to say, 'I've had my aerials removed, and it's quite painless.'

When we got down to the script, it soon became clear that the leading character of the play was becoming more and more like Malcolm himself, as he was eager to bring in his views not only about euthanasia but about all these other issues. I was the one who had to point this out to him, and it wasn't always easy; but in spite of a few storms we became very good friends, and the play was eventually produced with considerable success.

Opposite: plate 7 – 'The swamps, Wimbledon Common'

166

Chapter 19   A NEW DYNAMIC

ONE DAY we had a request from a Methodist District Chairman in Yorkshire asking us if we could help a young couple. Steve and Janet Stickley had left their jobs as drama teachers and were launching out with their own theatre company. It happened that their first performance was to be at Mitcham, quite near our home in Wimbledon, in the church of a young minister, Rob Frost. So on a night of thick snow we struggled through the blizzard to see them perform. They also had had difficulties in getting there, but on this very cold night with quite a small audience we watched them. They were quite outstanding.

One of their pieces was particularly brilliant, and we suggested that they should make it into a 40-minute lunchtime presentation for the Methodist Conference, which that year was being held at the Central Hall in London. We helped them with a director, Elizabeth Tooms, and finance and arranged for it to be given each day at St Margaret's in Parliament Square. It was a delightful sight to see the Rector of St Margaret's (shortly to become Bishop of Salisbury) in his shirt sleeves helping to get the stage up, as there was little time between the choir rehearsal and the first performance of the show.

About Face, as it was called, was largely a mime piece about the different masks people put on as they meet their boss, neighbours, wife, colleagues, etc. There is a dust man who wants to remove and collect the masks. He has a tough time of it, and ends by being thrown out of the third-storey window. When the office workers rush down to the street, they find he has gone, but he reappears at the end, in order to help the one man who has decided to get rid of his masks and talk honestly with his wife. One senior church woman said it had shaken her as nothing had ever done before and had made her aware of all the masks she wore.

Footprints, as their company is called, worked at first with no base and no funds, but 15 years later they are still

Opposite: Plate 8 – 'Autumn Trees'

going strong, having performed for tens of thousands of school children as well as in theatres and on television. Our partnership, which has gone on over the years, has included a co-production and tour of colleges with a play they wrote called *Zeal*, based on the true story of a Russian dissident. Phil and Rachel Hawthorn who played the leads in this are now doing very well working in BBC television. They and Steve and Janet have become two of our close friends and allies.

A most important event happened when one day at the Westminster Theatre we received a call from a Monsignor at Westminster Cathedral asking if he could come over and talk with us. This was Mgr George Leonard, Chaplain of the Catholic Stage Guild, Director of the Catholic Media Trust and advisor to the Cardinal. He brought over Michael Williams, Charles Pemberton, Kieron Moore and other figures in the theatre world.

'You have the only Christian theatre in the country,' he said, 'Can we work together?' To me this was one of the most marvellous moments I have experienced. When we had been in Italy several leaders of the Catholic Church had expressed themselves against our work, and although we did have friends in the Vatican, it had often made our work very difficult. Also here in Britain at one stage Catholics had been told not to involve themselves in MRA. So for this initiative to come from a prominent Catholic Monsignor who was close to the Cardinal was a wonderful step forward.

George Leonard was a great joy to work with. Outwardly a jolly, almost a Friar Tuck figure, we discovered he had great spiritual depth and a burning conviction about the importance of the Christian voice and influence in all the media.

This led to a very important development in the creation of a wider team. We had been holding one-day conferences for a wide range of people involved in the arts from all the mainline churches. Mgr Leonard felt that this was very important, and it was largely due to his conviction that these were expanded. So were started our Creative Conference weekends at Rodd, the home of Juliet Boobbyer's family, and later at Newick Park, the home of Lord and Lady Brentford. These drew together a wide range of people in the arts including prominent figures such as Christopher Fry, Malcolm Muggeridge and the writer Os Guiness.

These were very fruitful occasions, when our themes

*Monsignor George
Leonard*

were such subjects as 'The Prophetic Voice', 'The Art of
Affirmation', 'The Resurrection of the Imagination!',
'European Footprint', 'The Truth Shall Set You Free'.

Malcolm and Kitty Muggeridge often came to these
gatherings. I remember on one occasion after a talk by Os
Guiness, Malcolm in his usual style engaged in a lively de-
bate with him. At one point he referred to having been
married to Kitty for more than 40 years and added, 'Marry-
ing her was the best thing I ever did.' With dry humour
Kitty turned to him saying, 'Oh, I wish you'd told me that
before.' We subsequently had conferences in France and
in Switzerland and a major 10-day festival is now being
planned.

Working with George Leonard was also a personal en-
richment. He brought with him not only an acute intelli-
gence and judgement – he had been Public Affairs
Secretary to the Cardinal and also the force behind the re-
vitalisation of *The Universe* newspaper – but he also
brought a sense of the reality of the afterlife. I remember
after one session he took on prayer, Nancy Ruthven, an
actress and playwright and close friend, said to him, 'I
don't understand these realities in the way that you do.'
They had a talk together. Shortly afterwards Nancy was
killed in a fatal motor accident. George, although deeply
upset by this, said, 'Well, now she does understand.'

We all missed Nancy greatly, not only because she was
a delightful and original person and an accomplished actress and writer, but also because she held fast to her

169

commitment to affect the climate of opinion and values in the country through theatre and the media.

Over these years a very close and dedicated force of friends committed to 'moving the mountain' had been built up. Its strength was that we came from different backgrounds and disciplines. This meant that each enriched the others, producing a new dynamic of the Spirit.

Chapter 20   REBUILDING

DURING the years 1976 to 1986, Aldersgate was responsible for a great number of the plays with Christian content given in the Westminster Theatre. When there wasn't one of Aldersgate's plays available, the theatre was let out to other producers. It was in those years financially difficult to keep the theatre operation viable.

So after wide consultation it was agreed that Westminster Productions would expand. A new ecumenical board would be given a five-year period to run the theatre, under the chairmanship of Hugh Williams with new members, Mgr Leonard, Nigel Goodwin, Daniel Pearce, playwright Edmund Banyard, and a former United Reformed Church Moderator joining the Council. We started with revivals of *An Inspector Calls* and *The Miracle Worker*, but we began to realise that although some trusts were generous, there wasn't enough funding to carry this operation, and even more seriously, there weren't the new plays which would carry forward our purposes.

In order to begin to meet this latter need, we started a studio theatre in the building, which we called the First Floor Theatre with the aim of finding and encouraging new plays and playwrights. Under the excellent direction of Carol Henderson and John Locke, we ran two seasons and were hosts to some 16 different productions. This was an exciting and successful experiment, as it not only drew in new companies, but also attracted a young and enthusiastic audience and showed us one direction in which we should develop.

However, in 1990 this all came to an abrupt stop. A show due from America, *The Cotton Patch Gospel*, didn't arrive. We were badly let down and we were left with eight blank weeks. The Narnia plays, which had been making money, suddenly showed a loss due to new regulations for school parties, and Vaclav Havel's play *Temptation*, our most expensive production ever, proved to be a great disappointment and had to come off after a short run. It would seem, as one of our Board said, that the Lord was saying, 'Hold hard, I want you to go a different way.'

We found ourselves unable to continue. The theatre was handed back to the Oxford Group (MRA) and, most sadly of all, we had to cancel our next season of the studio theatre and make our staff redundant.

There was £70,000 worth of debts, which we were determined to honour. Many friends were very generous. We sold most of our lighting equipment and the last £7,000 I was able to raise through a month's painting exhibition in the Theatre foyer. So by January 1991 we were still solvent but having to start from scratch again. I often thought in those days of Kipling's lines:

> If you can meet with Triumph and Disaster
> And treat those two impostors just the same...
> Or watch the things you gave your life to, broken,
> And stoop and build 'em up with worn-out tools...

The truth is we weren't broken, but we had had a serious setback. We all learnt lessons from it. Mgr George Leonard wrote in *Westminster Theatre News* an article entitled *The Vision Lives On* which summarised what we all felt and was greatly encouraging. *(See Appendix 1)*

We had reached probably as many as four million people in this country. Many stones had been moved. Some of the plays had gone round the world, live or on video, and we now had this wonderful fellowship of friends taking on the same work.

But we were only at the beginning of our task. We believed that God's truth has to be portrayed through the arts of theatre and film, television and video, to reach the people of the modern world. To achieve this we have to find and encourage writers, designers, directors and producers who will do the job.

At the time of going to press with this book we are witnessing an exciting new development which could be the biggest step forward so far. Since 1992 a working party, comprised of representatives of all the Christian arts groups together with a representative of Churches Together in England, has been planning for the creation of a Christian Arts Centre in London. We see this as a real necessity: to have a focal point for all that is happening and should happen in these fields, a centre where new writers can be found, new productions encouraged, and from this centre reach out to the media here and abroad.

This could be the most important move in this area that we've ever made. Its success will depend a great deal on

172

the moral and financial support of the Christian people of the country.

The Christian Arts Trust which John Gibbs and I formed in 1982 and which has been greatly helped by our first two chairmen, the banker Derrick Hanson and Rev Dr Robert Latham, a former Moderator of the United Reformed Church, has become central to this move. It has helped to finance the initial work of the working group and also the feasibility studies which have been completed. Perhaps by the time this book is out, this may be another dream accomplished.

So the adventure goes on, and the core of people dedicated to this task will be joined by hundreds more in the next years.

PART IV

REFLECTIONS

Chapter 21 THE ROLE OF THE ARTS

Over these last 30 years I've come to the conclusion that the sovereignty of God is the crucial issue for individuals and countries. This brings one into conflict with the secular view that is the basis of much that is presented today. To live one's everyday life under that sovereignty demands an awareness of the essential truths about human existence, and these truths are also key ingredients of good theatre. In his book *The Everlasting Man* G K Chesterton noted that animals, fish and birds have many attributes, but only people have the gift of art. 'Art is the signature of man,' he concluded, 'because man is a unique creation of the Creator.'

In all the arts, including theatre, film and television, art's highest expression is attained when it reaches into every aspect of human experience, exploring the reality of a person's struggle to live faithful to his Creator and the universal moral laws, and to resist the pressures of ambition or fear. Art can enable us to understand and share the experiences of courage and cowardice, of hope and despair, which are all part of being human.

Whenever people have found some meaning in their lives they have used art to express it: Stone Age people with the paintings on the walls of their caves, the ancient Greeks in their dramas depicting the elemental issues of life and society, the Jewish people celebrating freedom in their festival of Passover, and others in their dances.

In the Christian era every advance in human life has been followed by some expression of that new life in one art form or another: the early Church's love feasts, the medieval monastery's illuminated manuscripts, and later the creation of great cathedrals, whose construction, sometimes taking hundreds of years, spoke in stone and glass of the glory of God.

Following the Franciscans and the new liberty of spirit came Giotto, the Renaissance and an outpouring of painting and sculpture.

This conflict between the sovereignty of God and our

own interests and desires lies at the heart of Shaw's *St Joan*. In Thornhill's play *Mr Wilberforce MP* the audience lives through his 30-year campaign against the slave trade, in the face of opposition, abuse, the forfeiting of high office and the lack of his wife's understanding. In Hugh Williams' *Poor Man, Rich Man* we feel the wonder of St Francis' faithfulness to his vision of a life free from the enslavement of possessions, despite the passionate longing for a family life.

All these plays portray the deepest truths about a human being's journey through life. This is not something that has to be justified or 'allowed' in drama, but is the very heart of drama and something which the greatest playwrights aim at.

It seems too that God is not only concerned with what we *do* to make 'Thy Kingdom come'; He seems to be even more concerned with what each of us *become*. And as I've found, what I do, the risks I take, have a great deal to do with what I become.

Chapter 22   THE ARTS OF PAINTING AND THEATRE

MY PAINTING has been a wonderful gift during the past 30 years. It takes my mind off the immediate issues of producing completely, and releases me for an hour or more. Often I would come home in the evening fairly worn out by the pressures, do an hour's painting, working from old sketches, and at the end of it be greatly refreshed.

It was after returning to England in 1963, that a friend of ours, Cynthia Scott Brown, was visiting us at our home in Wimbledon and seeing some of my paintings said, 'Can I buy two of these?' She then added, 'You ought to exhibit in the gallery in Church Road,' and gave me an introduction to the owner. Although he only sold one, that was the beginning of my moving into the professional field. I have been much aided by my son John, who helps with the frame cutting and with the accounts, and Mary, who puts the frames together and assembles the pictures.

I soon discovered that the way to sell was by holding one-man exhibitions and by getting a public figure to open them. These exhibitions were also a great help in raising money for the productions I was involved with. I would advertise it as a fund raising occasion, and then, being able to give £1,000 or more to that particular production, I could go with increased authority to trusts or businessmen and ask them to match what I was giving.

This also made it possible to get support from public figures, ranging from a member of the Government to well known personalities of theatre and film. I was delighted that the former Archbishop, Lord Coggan, with Lady Coggan, agreed to open one in our Wimbledon home.

These exhibitions were often held at the Westminster Theatre, sometimes in our home and also in various places around Britain. There have been 32 altogether. In June 1993 the actress Dame Thora Hird opened an exhibition of my paintings at the headquarters of the Arts Centre Group, then in Great Portland Street. During the course of this we naturally talked of our common interests in the theatre world.

*Lord and Lady Coggan opening an
exhibition of paintings
in the Mann's home*

I also mentioned my escape from prison camp and the part that the guidance of God had played in this. As a result she asked to interview me as part of her Sunday evening programme *Praise Be* which was recorded at our home in Wimbledon. Following this broadcast, which took place on 2nd May 1993, I received a letter forwarded from the BBC. It was from a man called John Woods who having seen the broadcast asked if I was the same Ron Mann who had been in Capua, Rezzonello and Fontanellato camps, because if I was he had a portrait of himself which I had painted in 1943. This also had been lost for a year, taken to Germany by a fellow prisoner of war, and finally returned to him.

Shortly after I received the letter, I had the pleasure of meeting him again and of seeing the portrait, which I'm pleased to say was a very good likeness.

Thora Hird filming at the Mann's home in Wimbledon

180

*Picture of John Woods
painted in 1943*

Another exhibition was at Bentalls store in Kingston upon Thames, kindly arranged by Rowan Bentall, the Chairman. Before the occasion my family said, 'You must do some local scenes.' I went out and began to explore and thus discovered the wonders of Wimbledon Common and the Thames between Richmond and Ham which have since become two of my favourite painting spots. Almost as Bernard Eyre-Walker had a place where he went when the light was not particularly exciting, so I go to the swamps or other parts of the Common and nearly always find something delightful there. Plates no 7 *(facing page 166)*, and 8 *(facing page 167)* are two of my latest paintings. I've painted on that stretch near Ham a score of times and even more often done simple impressions of the trees and water there, as in Plate no 9 *(facing page 182)*. To discover a certain magic in familiar scenes nearby is perhaps as important as exploring the beauty of the fells of Lakeland or the Scottish Highlands. Trying to express that 'other dimension' – the realities of the human condition, the wonder of life – has become my major concern.

After the struggle of producing in the theatre, to go north to the Lakeland fells has been a re-charging of batteries, a moving out into a different world. Part of its recreative power is that painting is so absorbing. I have on occasion been on the fells sitting on an inflatable cushion on the snow and after an hour or so have stood up and wobbled, suddenly realising that my feet had gone completely dead with the cold.

Just occasionally I have managed to convey something of what I feel. One such moment was whilst sitting in the snow, although this time it wasn't possible to paint as the snow showers kept coming over. We had parked our car at the top of Honister Pass, and then decided to go right up the steep side to Grey Knotts as it was cold and snowing, but then rather regretted having taken that route as it was steeper than we had thought. Once on the top we went along those delightful fells from which you can see at different times into Borrowdale, Buttermere and Ennerdale and finally stopped on the side of Brandreth looking towards Great Gable.

It kept snowing intermittently, and we ate our sandwiches and had hot tea from the thermos, sitting on a rock looking towards Gable.

Suddenly there came a break in the clouds, and the sun shone on to the snow-covered side of the mountain. I made a quick pencil sketch and a note of the colours and later that day was able to capture something of that magical moment. *(Plate no 10)*

One of my chief delights during the last few years has been to go out with Heaton Cooper to some of his favourite spots. Although I'd been over Wrynose Pass and Hardknott many times, and often stopped on Wrynose to go up to a favourite spot of Red Tarn, I'd never stopped on the top of Hardknott. There is very little room to park there, but we found a place, as Heaton said that the top of the fell is one of the most glorious spots in Lakeland. So together we went up several times and found it all that he had said.

The day I remember most is when Mary and I went without him on a very bright day, and I started to paint towards Bowfell with long shadows coming down the fell side. Then as the sun came round, I painted towards the south. Harter Fell had a lovely cerulean blue tint, and there was a pool reflecting the colour in the foreground. Mary said, 'Have you looked the other way?', so I turned round, and Sca Fell was bathed in a violet light and below you could see the upper Eskdale Valley threading its way up towards Esk Hause. So I started the third painting of that day. It was only a rough attempt, but later I worked from that sketch and finished one of the paintings I'm most pleased with *(Plate no 12)*.

The last time we were staying with Heaton was in June

Opposite : Plate 9 – 'The Thames at Ham'
Centre left: Plate 10 – 'Great Gable in snow'
Centre right: Plate 11 – 'Scafell from Border End'
Facing page 183: Plate 12 – 'Crummock Water'

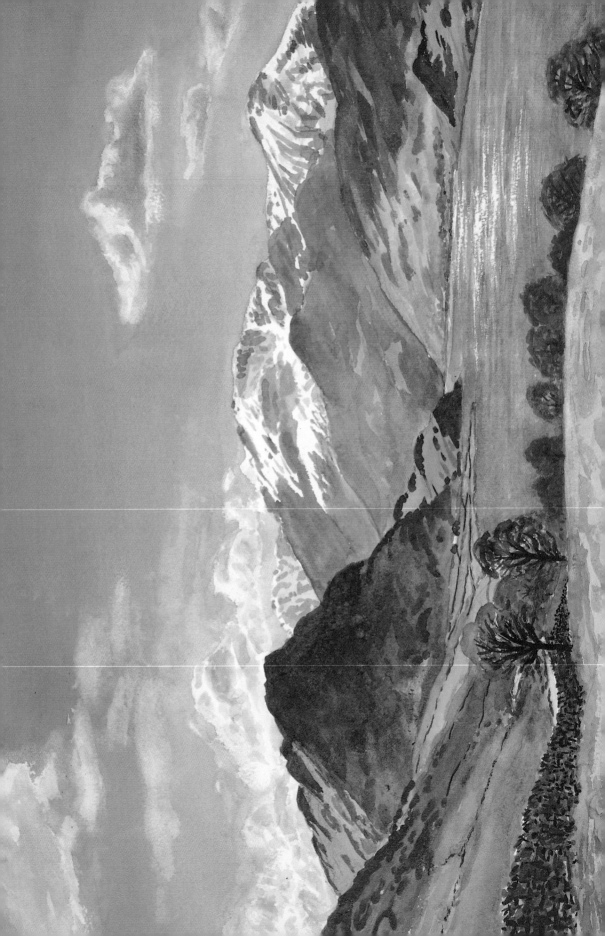

With Heaton Cooper at the side of Crummock Water

1992, and I asked, 'Where would you like to go?' 'Crummock', he replied, 'although I'm not sure I can manage the walk down from Low Park to the lake side.' However, he did manage it, and sat in the very cold wind to do yet another painting. Looking up Crummock is Rannerdale Knott and Green and Great Gable at the far end. For both of us this is a treasured spot. Heaton spent his honeymoon there, and it was the place where I met up again with him and Ophelia when I got back from prison camp. I'm never tired of painting it in all its different moods, but especially with snow on the fells.

On this particular day we called in to see the friends who live in Low Park, Bob and Margot Watkins. It's been almost a tradition in the past years to call in on Margot's mother, Beth Alexander, who would entertain us in an old-world, gracious manner to tea. *Plate no 12* was painted during one of our stays there. They have become close friends, especially as Bob's twin brother whom I met in London became the Treasurer of both Aldersgate and the Christian Arts Trust.

Sometimes when I've asked Heaton, 'Where shall we go?' he has said Coniston, which is special to him because he was brought up there. So we've painted together many times from the east side of the lake or from Torver looking towards Coniston, Old Man and Dow Crag. What is always surprising is the different feel that each of us gets even when painting from a similar angle, but we both sell them equally well, although not surprisingly Heaton gets much higher prices.

183

An extra pleasure for me has been to do a painting on a large card for some of my friends. Also sometimes when a friend is seriously ill, one is able to say something in a painting better than in words. Geoffrey Daukes, whom I had known for many years, had been told that he had not many weeks to live, and I painted a scene based on the Fleetwood coastline for him. It was inspired by the lines from that wonderful hymn of Whittier's with two verses that go:

> And so beside the silent sea
> I wait the muffled oar;
> No harm from Him can come to me
> On ocean or on shore.

> I know not where his islands lift
> Their fronded palms in air;
> I only know I cannot drift
> Beyond His love and care.

In a life of great activity, geared generally to running a company, producing plays, and organising and assisting conferences, it is very easy to miss out the elements of

Beside the silent sea

wonder and of worship. The painting part of my life has supplied much of those elements, when one becomes conscious of the hand behind it all, the other dimension to life which was so vivid to George Leonard. I am always greatly heartened when people say to me that a painting they have bought provides something of that element in their lives.

Heaton Cooper opening an exhibition at the Westminster Theatre

Photo: D Loughman

En plein air...

Chapter 23   ADVENTURE OF FAITH

IT WILL soon be 50 years since I resigned my secure job with the Lancashire County Council, my only financial security being a small army disability pension because of my damaged eye.

Since then I haven't received any salary and yet we've survived. Whilst in the USA and South America and in Italy we pooled our resources, sharing what we had individually and living on money given for the work we were doing. In Italy we were quite often short of funds and had to live very frugally. With St Paul I can say, 'I know what it is to be brought low, and I know what it is to have plenty.'

When Mary and I and our son John arrived back in England in 1963 we had £2,000 of savings, and our only income was the interest from this and my pension. As we had nowhere to live we were most grateful that some friends of ours, Dr and Mrs Mackay, offered us, rent-free, the first floor of their home in Wimbledon. After Dr Mackay died we helped to look after his widow for a year or two. Then his son and family felt that they should move in and look after their mother.

We then had a very clear thought, in a time of quiet, that we should buy a house, and that we should invite my sister Dorothy and my mother to join us, when my sister retired from her headmistress's job four years later.

Dorothy and Mother were very pleased at the thought that we should make a family home together. So Dorothy came down to London and said that she would take on finding half the money needed.

After looking at one or two houses we went to see a house in West Wimbledon, a three-storey, four-bed-roomed, semi-detached that was up for sale. Immediately we felt this was the right house and because there was someone else already eager to buy it, we had to make up our minds quickly – the same day that we saw it.

This was an act of faith because although Dorothy could get a mortgage for her share of the property, we had no possibility of that or of finding the money needed. However, our clear thought was to tell the agent that we would buy it, assuring him that there was no problem with the money.

The price of the house was £8,950 – this was 1969.

The most wonderful point was that the owner, who was a builder, having tried and failed to get planning permission for the very large bottom half of the garden, included this quarter-acre plot in the sale of the house.

As we were in process of signing the agreement, to our surprise and delight close friends of ours came up with a very generous offer: they would loan us £5,000, interest free, to be repaid when Dorothy and I sold the Fleetwood house. So we moved into 65 Cambridge Road, and during the four years until Mother and Dorothy joined us, we were able to let the top floor of the house which gave us enough income to meet our expenses. In 1973 when we sold the Fleetwood house we were able to repay the loan and Dorothy repaid her mortgage. Dorothy, having retired after 30 very effective years as a headmistress, and Mother then in her 80's, joined us.

Over the years we have received many gifts from family and friends. Although Mary at that time had a share in the family estate trust, this did not produce any income except once, when in 1974 the trustees all shared in the proceeds of the sale of three farms.

In 1987 our son John bought a house in Milton Keynes, and as Dorothy had recently had a stroke the three-storey house was becoming more difficult for us, so we decided to see if we could get planning permission for the bottom part of our garden. This was granted, and with the wonderful help of an architect friend, Rosemary Harris, we were able to build what for us is a dream house, surrounded by an orchard and with a studio-cum-guestroom and lots of room for entertaining.

So by selling 65 Cambridge Road we found ourselves, sharing with Dorothy, in a new bungalow and with money left over for us to live on – really enough for the first time in our married lives. I remember saying, 'What have we done to deserve this blessing!'

So we have reason to believe the words of Jesus when he says, 'There is no one who has given up home... or land for my sake who will not receive in this age a hundred times as much.' It may be just a coincidence, but in the years since I have taken full responsibility for the finances of all the work I was engaged in, our own personal needs have been taken care of.

I wanted to set out these facts because many of my

friends, especially in the theatre world, are sceptical when I tell them I've received no salary (and hardly any expenses) from MRA. Although I was offered a salary when we formed Aldersgate, I didn't accept it as I knew we would never survive as a company if I took a producer's salary from it. But this is how it has worked out. Earnings from my painting, although mostly given away for productions, have enabled us to pay for further painting trips. For those who remain sceptical, I say that this has also been the experience of many of my friends today as well as the experience of many over the centuries.

Perhaps the greatest joy is the constant flow of people through our house in both large parties and small, which I believe already gives the home its particular character. Some call it an oasis. One of our biggest delights is to entertain our West Indian friends from Bridge Park and our friends from Broadwater Farm.

LISTENING

The decision I made 60 years ago to take time each day to listen to God has been a tremendous aid. Perhaps my journey of faith is summed up in the words of Whittier's hymn:

> All as God wills, who wisely heeds
> To give or to withhold,
> And knoweth more of all my needs
> Than all my prayers have told.
>
> Enough that blessings undeserved
> Have marked my erring track;
> That whereso'er my feet have swerved,
> His chastening turned me back;
>
> That care and trial seem at last,
> Through memory's sunset air,
> Like mountain ranges overpast,
> In purple distance fair;
>
> And so the shadows fall apart,
> And so the west winds play;
> And all the windows of my heart
> I open to the day.

189

Appendix 1   THE VISION LIVES ON

Mgr Leonard wrote in the *Westminster Theatre News*:

'A vision once shared has a life of its own. It might be frustrated by adverse circumstances for a while, but it survives and continues to inspire. When the time is right it can blossom again into fresh forms and new beauty.

'Those of us who have struggled against the odds to create a vibrant and viable Christian theatre in the heart of London are gripped by such a vision. Now, with the utmost reluctance, Westminster Productions has been forced to abandon for a while its present dream ...

'The board members of Westminster Productions came from widely different backgrounds but shared a common dream. It grew out of forty years of brave and often lonely pioneering by Moral Re-armament. The movement's enthusiasm and faith shaped the theatre. It was the significance of drama in the battle to win minds and hearts. Of recent years, MRA recognised that new situations require new solutions. Generously – sacrificially even – it entrusted its theatre, and provided considerable financial backing, to a new board representing all the mainstream Christian churches. For that Westminster Productions will remain forever grateful.

'Our board believed – and still unrepentantly does – that to help our generation find its soul it must be offered a theatre and a school of writing and performance which celebrate and enrich the human spirit. We did not set out to moralise or berate; we saw little value in merely re-counting improving stories; our aim remains that of affirming all that is truly and profoundly human.

'Naturally any avowedly Christian theatre is fiercely resented by those who feel threatened by its convictions. It would be naive to expect critical acclaim from today's liberal and permissive establishment. Unfortunately we also failed to convince committed Christians of the crucial importance of imagination and creativity in the service of truth...

'Failure, however, is never fatal. Fellowship forged in a shared endeavour will survive ...

'At the moment God's purposes remain unclear. But the vision lives on.'

Last year at our AGM, he gave us the benefit of his experience and thinking on the task of communicating with this generation. Here are some extracts from his talk:

'It is not surprising, when we stop to think about it, that God's revelation to his people in both the Old and the New Testaments is not a series of teachings and propositions, but a story of salvation, a history, about people; and what teaching there is is often poetic, imaginative, and contained in parables. Usually it is left to the listener to draw the moral, to point out the meaning. Only to the inner circle is the full meaning revealed. Nor is it surprising that theatre and drama have their roots in religion. The drama of ancient Greece, the mystery plays of the Middle Ages, were a way of entering into a sacred experience: they did not necessarily have a sacred theme; they always had an experience of the sacred. A Christian believer sees God in all creation and in all human experience; there is always the sacred at the heart of things. I have a feeling that when people talk about the magic of the theatre they are dimly sensing the religious origins and function of drama; in a secular way they are sharing the experience of being human, they are purging themselves of fear and anger and emerging in some way charged and renewed. And that is religious ...

'I have stressed these fundamental ideas rather than the structure and institution of the Westminster Theatre becase I believe intensely that the vision is more important than the place and that our first priority must be people and ideas and not bricks and mortar. The Westminster is a vision, a creative community, much more than it is a building, however beloved, however well equipped.

'But some kind of flagship, some visible centre is, of course, essential. Where else but here could the *First Floor Theatre* have taken off – and how, without a venue, can experimental, unknown plays be tried out and developed? Without this centre and those creative spirits who were drawn to it, how could the Creative Conferences have developed and brought together kindred souls? Without the Westminster the various seminars and symposia on broadcasting and television could never have been organised. The Westminster Theatre has made its distinctive contribution but it is now crystal clear that God is calling us to fold our pilgrim tent and find new ways of making our vision live.

'One door has closed; we await others to open...'

192

Appendix 2   THEATRICAL PRODUCTIONS

The author was producer, co-producer or promoter of the following plays.

ALDERSGATE PRODUCTIONS LTD

1976   *Ride! Ride!* book and lyrics by Alan Thornhill   May 20 - June 24
with Gordon Gostelow, Caroline Villiers, Brendan Barry.
Music by Penelope Thwaites
Directed by Peter Coe
(Touring previously from March 2 to Nottingham, Leeds,
Newcastle, Bradford, Hull, Liverpool, Manchester,
Birmingham, Wolverhampton, Bristol, Southampton.)

1977   *Three Christian Plays*
Presented by Aldersgate Productions
in collaboration with the Greater London Churches Council.

    Fire by Hugh Steadman Williams   March 8 - 28
One Friday by Edmund Banyard   March 29 - April 16
with Ruth Madoc
Brother Francis by Peter Albery & William Fry   April 19 - May 7
Theatre Roundabout Production

1978   *Sentenced To Life* by Malcolm Muggeridge and Alan Thornhill   May 17 - July 22
Directed by David William

1980   *Song of the Lion* by Daniel Pearce   September 25 - October 18
based on the life and writings of C S Lewis
with Hugh Manning as C S Lewis
Produced by Ronald Mann and John Gibbs.
Directed by David William
(Premiere at the Ludlow Festival then toured Oxford
 Cambridge, Ipswich, Birmingham, Chichester Festival,
 Brighton.)

1981   *Song of the Lion*   January 15 - February 7
Reopened at Westminster Theatre

1981-82   *Gavin and the Monster* by Hugh Steadman Williams   November 17 - January 23
Music by Kathleen Johnson
Directed by Denise Coffey

1984-85   *The Lion, the Witch, and the Wardrobe* by C S Lewis   November 20 - January 15
Adapted for stage by Glyn Robbins
Directed by Richard Williams

A joint production of Aldersgate, Westminster and
Vanessa Ford Productions.
(It then toured the country to the following theatres:
Kings, Edinburgh; Opera House, Belfast; Grand,
Wolverhampton; Apollo, Oxford; Grand, Swansea;
Palace, Manchester; Forum, Billingham; Hippodrome,
Bristol; Kings, Southsea;Theatre Royal, Plymouth;
Opera House, Buxton; Opera House, Blackpool;
Hippodrome, Birmingham; His Majesty's, Aberdeen;
Lyceum, Crewe; Congress, Eastbourne; Pavilion, Bourne-
mouth; Gaiety, Douglas, Isle of Man; Forum,Billingham;
Theatre Royal, Bath; Hexagon, Reading;The Beck,
Hillingdon; Marlowe, Canterbury; Derngate,Northampton;
Theatre Royal, Norwich; Alhambra, Bradford.)

1985	*Man of Two Worlds* by Daniel Pearce	April 25 - July 1
1985-86	*The Lion, the Witch and the Wardrobe* (It again toured 25 regional theatres.) 108 performances	November 18 - January 20
1986	*The Lion, the Witch and the Wardrobe* (Followed by nationwide tour)	November 24 - January 19
1987	*The Lion, the Witch and the Wardrobe* (Followed by nationwide tour)	November 11 - January 18
1987-88	*The Voyage of the Dawntreader* by C S Lewis (Followed by nationwide tour)	December 23 - February 6
1988	*The Miracle Worker* by William Gibson with Hildegard Neil, Ian Lavender, Daryl Back as Helen Keller. Directed by Adrian Reynolds	March 9 - June 30
1988	*The Magician's Nephew* by C S Lewis	November 20 - Dec 24
1988-89	*The Lion, the Witch and the Wardrobe* (These two plays did a nationwide tour together.)	December 26 - February 4
1989-90	*The Magician's Nephew*	December 5 - January 6
1989-90	*The Lion, the Witch and the Wardrobe* (These two productions then did a nationwide tour together. These tours which went on for more than five years were very ably managed by our partners, Vanessa Fordand Glyn Robbins, and were seen by more than one and a half million people.)	January 16 - February 2

WESTMINSTER PRODUCTIONS LTD

1963-64	*The Diplomats* by Peter Howard	December 31 165 performances
1964	*Mr Brown Comes Down the Hill* – a modern murder story by Peter Howard (This play has since been filmed for television.)	May 28 212 performances
1964-65 1st Year	*Give a Dog a Bone* – pantomime with book and lyrics by Peter Howard Music by George Fraser Design by W Cameron Johnson Costumes by Dorothy Phillips	Christmas
1965	*Mr Wilberforce MP* – historical play by Alan Thornhill Design by W Cameron Johnson. (Toured to: Newcastle, Hull, Manchester, Bradford, Belfast, Cardiff, Bath.) (277 schools sent parties to see this play.)	February 11 195 performances
1965-66	*Give a Dog a Bone* (2nd year) (For two months over Christmas season)	December 9
1966	*The Dictator's Slippers* by Peter Howard and *The Ladder* by Peter Howard	April 7-May 23
1966/67	*Give a Dog a Bone* (3rd year) (For two months over Christmas season) (Filmed under direction of Henry Cass in 1966)	December 8
1967	*Happy Deathday* by Peter Howard For eight weeks	February 9
1967	*Annie* – musical with book and lyrics by Alan Thornhill with Bill Kenwright, Angela Richards. Music by William L Reed	July 27 - December 9
1967-68	*Give a Dog a Bone* (4th year)	December 14 -January 27
1968	*Annie* (continued)	February 1 -August 31
1968	*Bishop's Move* by Alan Thornhill Directed by Henry Cass Design by W Cameron Johnson	September 12 - Dec 7
1968-69	*Give a Dog a Bone* (5th year) (For two months over Christmas season)	December 12
1969	*Hide Out* by Alan Thornhill	March 7 - May 24

1969	*High Diplomacy* – musical, with book and lyrics by Alan Thornhill and Hugh Steadman Williams with Muriel Smith, Donald Scott. Music by George Fraser and William L Reed	June 5 - November 1
1969-70	*Give a Dog a Bone* (6th year) (For two months over Christmas season)	December 11
1970	*Blindsight* by Anne Wolrige Gordon with Sharon Duce, Joyce Heron, Michael Malnick.	May 28 - November 28 July 2 - November 28
1970	*The Forgotten Factor* by Alan Thornhill with Philip Friend	July 2 7 week run
1970-71	*Give a Dog a Bone* (7th year) with Tony Jackson, Lon Satton. (For two months over Christmas season)	December 10
1971-72	*Give a Dog a Bone* (8th year) with Donald Scott, Tony Jackson. (For two months over Christmas season)	Christmas
1972	*Cross Road* – multi-media experiment, the Frank Buchman story Created by Ailsa Hamilton, Juliet Boobbyer, Ronald Mann. Directed by Hugh Steadman Williams, Valerie Fleming. (Toured the country and then was made into a film.)	May 4 - July 22 & September 28 - Nov 25
1972-73	*Give a Dog a Bone* (9th year) (For two months over Christmas season)	Christmas
1973	*GB* by Alan Thornhill, Michael Henderson and Hugh Steadman Williams. Music by Kathleen Johnson	March 6 - June 30
1973-74	*Give a Dog a Bone* (10th year) (For two months over Christmas season)	Christmas
1974-75	*Give a Dog a Bone* (11th year – final production) For two months over Christmas season	December 5 - February 1
1975	*Return Trip* by Alan Thornhill and Hugh Steadman Williams	June 16 - July 10
1978	*Love All* – musical entertainment about Bunny Austin and Phyllis Konstam by Nancy Ruthven and Tony Jackson with Ruth Madoc, Brogden Miller.	October 26 - November 18
1979	*Poor Man, Rich Man* – one-man show based on the life of St Francis of Assisi by Hugh Steadman Williams with Michel Orphelin as St Francis. Music by Kathleen Johnson	June 24 only

Musical Director: John Burrows
Directed by John Dryden
(This then toured UK, France, Belgium,
Switzerland, Germany, Canada, USA and Philippines.)

1979	*Stranger in the House* by Hugh Steadman Williams with John Locke and Chris Channer Directed by Nancy Ruthven	September 10 - October 5
1980	*Ragman* by Edmund Banyard Music by Frances Campbell	February 25 - March 22
1980	*Mr Wilberforce MP* by Alan Thornhill (Produced for A Day of London Theatre)	September 23 - October 18
1981	*The Namesake* by Nancy Ruthven From the novels by C Walter Hodges Music by Kathleen Johnson and William L Reed	March 3 - 28
1981	*Jonas* by Daniel Pearce (Produced for A Day of London Theatre)	October 6 - 24
1981-82	*Gavin and the Monster* by Hugh Steadman Williams Music by Kathleen Johnson Directed by Denise Coffey Co-producer: Aldersgate Productions Ltd	November 17 - January 23
1982	*An Inspector Calls* by J B Priestley with Chris Channer, Philip Tyndale-Biscoe. Directed by John Blatchley (Produced for A Day of London Theatre)	March 2 -27
1987	*An Inspector Calls* by J B Priestley with Tom Baker, Peter Baldwin, Pauline Jameson, Charlotte Attenborough. Co-producer: Aldersgate Productions Ltd (For three months)	May 6
1989	*An Ideal Husband* by Oscar Wilde Directed by Patrick Sandford	April 18 - November 25
1990	*Temptation* by Vaclav Havel Translated from the Czech by George Theiner with Sylvester McCoy, Frank Middlemass, Aden Gillett, Rula Lenska. Directed by James Roose-Evans Produced by Hugh Steadman Williams	June 6 - July 14

FIRST FLOOR THEATRE – FIRST SEASON

The First Floor Theatre was initiated by the author
and other Council members of Westminster Productions Ltd.

1989	*Beauty and the Bounders* – Polly March	September 19 - 30
	Dance of a Woman Warrior – Peri Aston	October 17 - 21
	I Spy – Trapdoor Theatre	October 24 - 25
	The Letter – Ann Clifford	October 26 - 28
	Paul Jones and Fiona Hendley	November 1
	Oxford Circus – juggling, sword fighting	November 2
	Liverpool poets – Roger McGough, Brian Patten and Stewart Henderson	November 3
	Music and Storytelling – Mary O'Hara	November 4
	The Widening Gyre – Nancy Ruthven	November 7 - 25

FIRST FLOOR THEATRE – SECOND SEASON

1990	*Sacred Elephant* – Virginia McKenna	April 17 - 21
	To Sea in a Sieve – Brian Sibley and Polly March	April 24 - May 5
	Poor Man, Rich Man – Hugh Steadman Williams	May 8 - 19
	The Letter – Ann Clifford	May 22 - 26
	Arms and the Boy – Arts Arena	May 29 - 30
	China Dolls – Danny Scott	May 31
	The World's a Stage I'm Going Through – Milton Jones	June 1 - 2
	The First Stone – AGAPE Theatre Company	June 5 - 6
	Counter-Balance – Springs Dance Company, poetry by Stewart Henderson, with Carol Henderson.	June 7 - 9